The Knock at
the Door

The Knock at the Door

THREE GOLD STAR FAMILIES
BONDED BY GRIEF AND PURPOSE

Ryan Manion
Heather Kelly
Amy Looney Heffernan

CENTER
STREET

New York   Nashville

Center Stree
Hachette Book Group
1290 Avenue of the Americas, New York, NY 10104
centerstreet.com
twitter.com/centerstreet

First Edition: November 2019

Center Street is a division of Hachette Book Group, Inc. The Center Street name and logo are trademarks of Hachette Book Group, Inc.

The publisher is not responsible for websites (or their content) that are not owned by the publisher.

The Hachette Speakers Bureau provides a wide range of authors for speaking events. To find out more, go to www.HachetteSpeakersBureau.com or call (866) 376-6591.

Library of Congress Cataloging-in-Publication Data has been applied for.

ISBNs: 978-1-5460-8523-2 (hardcover), 978-1-5460-8522-5 (ebook)

Printed in the United States of America

LSC-C

10 9 8 7 6 5 4 3 2 1

*To all Gold Star mothers, fathers,
husbands, wives, sisters, brothers,
sons, and daughters*

Contents

The Knock at
the Door

★ ★ ★

The Knock at the Door

L ike most Americans of a certain age, I remember exactly where I was just before 9 a.m. on September 11, 2001. I was in bed in my apartment at Widener University, just outside Philadelphia.

I woke up to a panicky call from my mom, who was at my childhood home in Doylestown, Pennsylvania. She had just heard from my brother, Travis, who was a student at the United States Naval Academy in Annapolis. He had called to tell her that he was okay and that he and the rest of the student body were being moved to an undisclosed location and would not be in contact for a bit. One minute she was listening to his intense but measured voice, and the next—*click*—the voice was gone.

As a mother now, I can't imagine receiving a call like that. My mom had first tried to reach my dad, but after a few failed attempts, she called me instead. I was still groggy from sleep and couldn't make much sense of what she was saying, but it was clear that she was upset. She instructed me to turn on the nearest TV. I did, and a minute later we watched together in horror as the second plane struck the World Trade Center. We spent the next several minutes in silence, each watching the events unwind on the television in front of us.

A few minutes later, I hung up the phone and wondered what I was supposed to do next. When I think back to that terrible day, I remember the horror and sadness the most. Those are the strongest feelings that have stayed with me through the years.

What I often forget, until I reflect a little, were the feelings of total and utter confusion. You have to remember that this was a totally unprecedented national event. I literally thought the world was coming to an end. I looked to others helplessly for some direction on how to respond. There was no playbook for this.

I tried to think rationally about what my next move should be. Do I go to my parents' house? Do I keep watching and try to understand the severity of the incident? Do I call around and see who else knows what to do next? How can I help? I took my cues from the other students around me. While most were dumbstruck, none of them appeared personally threatened. So I decided to go to English class.

When I got there I saw that my professor had the TV on and was listening intently to the reporters. They were saying that the attack was an act of terrorism. At the time, I barely knew what that word meant. Since then, of course, the term *terrorism* has become a ubiquitous presence in our national lexicon.

Then my professor asked each of us to pull out a blank piece of paper and write down whatever thoughts were going through our heads in that moment. I exchanged glances with a few nearby students, and their expressions seemed to confirm what I was feeling: History was unfolding around us.

I took a deep breath and, as instructed, allowed my thoughts to pour out onto the paper. I wrote about how scared I was for my dad, who was then serving in the military, and for my brother, who was about to serve in the military. I wrote about my fear that what was happening—whatever it was—would lead to war and that they would have to play some role in that.

A few years ago, while cleaning out an old box packed with textbooks and notebooks from college, I found that piece of paper. I scanned it and remembered the confusion we all felt that day. We wondered what these horrific acts meant for our futures, both as individuals and as a country. My eyes moved to the last line that I had written: "I just hope nothing happens to my dad or Travis. I don't think I'd be able to go on if it did."

After his graduation from the Naval Academy, Travis was commissioned as an officer in the US Marine Corps. Six years after I wrote down my worries in that English class, they were realized. Travis was killed in Iraq on April 29, 2007.

The news of Travis's death started with a knock at my family's front door. Outside stood a uniformed service member who had been tasked with telling a family that their son and brother was dead. It's one of the hardest jobs I can imagine. I'm one of thousands of family members who have learned of their loved one's death in this same way. None of us saw it coming. All of us were gutted to the core. After the uniformed messengers leave and the families and friends go back to their lives, we're left to pick up the pieces; to use my phrase from college, we're forced to find a way to "go on."

And I'll tell you what, it's not always pretty.

The struggles and triumphs of life never are, though. This book is for those of you who have ever had to answer a life-changing knock at the door—real or metaphorical. You know how ugly things can get. And if you haven't yet answered one, I promise you, you will.

You may not experience the gut-wrenching loss of a loved one to war, but knocks come in all different forms. Maybe it's a cancer diagnosis. Maybe it's the death of your best friend. The betrayal of a spouse. The loss of a child. The implosion of a professional career. A car accident or natural disaster that takes the person you love the most away from you.

In each case, the circumstances are different, but the principles are the same. We are unexpectedly robbed of something or someone we loved. We are stripped down to the rawest versions of ourselves and forced to take a look in the mirror.

As we seek to cope, to respond, to "go on," we inevitably come to a point where we determine what kind of person we will be: the kind who is broken by tragedy, the kind who is defined by it, or the kind who is strengthened by it. Grief is a process, of course, and at times we're all three. The trick is remembering that we control this process, and that our experiences can teach us something critical, if we let them.

It took me several years to figure this out. That is, I finally learned to accept grief as a fluid process and not a hurdle I had to push through. And I came to understand that I actually got a say in its outcome. Fortunately, I've had the help of a few good friends to push me along toward the other side. Two of those friends have chosen to co-author this book with me and have shared what they learned from their experiences of tragedy as well.

We are three women whose loved ones were torn from us before we reached the age of thirty. I'd like to be able to say that we're unique and that our experiences are isolated, but that's not true. Thousands of people have suffered the loss of a loved one in service, and millions more have experienced some other unexpected and tragic knock at their front doors.

This book is for them. It's for anyone who has negotiated struggle, grief, and pain, and emerged stronger as a result. It's for anyone who is fighting that battle right now and may be tempted to give up.

Neither I nor my co-authors, Amy Looney Heffernan and Heather Kelly, pretend to have all the answers. We're very much a work in progress ourselves. But we think we've stumbled on a few good pieces of wisdom. And if by sharing that hard-earned wisdom, we can help just one person find comfort, growth, or affirmation in a difficult time, then we'll consider our time more than well spent.

Amy, Heather, and I have a friendship that goes back several years. We're an unlikely trio in a lot of ways, and in an alternate universe, we may never even have become friends. But tragedy brings with it unintended consequences. Travis's death deprived me of my best friend, but it also provided me with new and meaningful relationships I couldn't have anticipated and for which I am exceedingly grateful. Amy and Heather are two examples of this. The three of us are bound by grief and by loss, and by the special relationship we have with a small plot of land outside Washington.

In the southeast corner of Arlington National Cemetery lies Section 60, where the remains of those who have died most recently in the service of our country are laid to rest. It is an especially peaceful place. Whether it's an early spring morning and the grass is still wet with dew, or a crisp autumn afternoon and leaves, caught by a gust of wind, swirl among the white marble headstones—there is a tranquility here that can be found nowhere else.

This is only fitting. The men and women who lie buried here have earned their right to peace. They chose war as their profession. When the dead of Section 60 signed up to fight, they knew they weren't fighting for any politician or political agenda. They were fighting for a nation, for a set of ideals, and for principles that they knew were bigger than themselves or any party or leader. They signed up to stand guard over their fellow Americans' rights to vote, to pray, to learn, and to love in safety.

That's what our loved ones signed up to defend, and that's what they died defending. Amy and Heather lost their husbands, and I lost my brother. Today the three men lie within a couple rows of one another in the quiet confines of Section 60. My brother, Travis Manion, and Amy's late husband, Brendan Looney, are buried next to each other, honoring the bond they forged together at the US Naval Academy. After they graduated, Travis became a Marine and Brendan became a Navy SEAL.

Travis died in a firefight in Iraq; Brendan died in a helicopter crash in Afghanistan. Now they rest side by side.

A few rows away is Heather's husband, Rob Kelly, who followed in his father's footsteps and became a Marine. Rob didn't know Brendan or Travis, but there is a cold logic to his burial nearby. He was killed less than three months after Brendan, and the graves were filled in order of casualties received.

The three of us have all spent time below these sloping hills, both together and alone. At first, these visits were solemn and tear-filled. We'd spend hours sitting in the grass by their graves. Some bystanders would stare blankly; others would look on in sorrow.

We each had our own rituals. We brought mementos to place on their headstones—pictures of us together, a Marine Corps Marathon medal, rocks from a trip to Hawaii. In the early months and years, we visited in order to make sure we checked in with Travis, Brendan, and Rob, to include them in our lives as they went on. For a long time, it was a formal ritual of somber reflection.

Visiting the graves in Section 60 is no longer as ritualistic to us as it once was. These days, when we make the trip, it's not so much a ceremonial rite as it is a comforting visit. And it isn't as somber anymore, either. It's an occasion to gather with friends and family to celebrate our loved ones. We still feel them around us there, but in the years since we lost them, they have inspired us to go on living our lives, to do so much more.

This book details the unlikely routes that our three lives took, and the even more unlikely ways in which our lives came to intersect. It's the story of what happens after the flag-draped caskets come home from battle, and what becomes of the families who are left behind in the wake of war.

But more than anything, it's the story of what is possible when you commit to living your life with a resilient spirit—whatever the struggle you may be facing, and whatever the difficulty that may be knocking at the door. Because hurt is hurt and pain is pain. There is no point in comparing our tragedies. Who wants to measure one person's cancer diagnosis against another's addiction against another's trauma? As if that's a game that anyone wants to win anyway. We all have difficulties to overcome, and in my opinion, they are commensurate with the absolute maximum we can handle. Whatever you see as your limit, you will be pushed to it. In most cases, you will be pushed *over* it. So then what do you do?

That's what happened to each of us, and this book is our attempt to answer that question.

Nearly a year ago, Amy, Heather, and I were asked to share our stories of loss and struggle in a very public forum. We were invited to interview together on *CBS This Morning* for a news piece that would be aired to millions of viewers across the country.

Each of us responded in a way that aligned with our personality. I, of course, was the most gung ho of the group, ready to jump in and start tackling some hard-hitting issues and eager to share with America our stories and those of Travis, Brendan, and Rob.

Easygoing Amy was amused at the prospect. I think she laughed out loud in disbelief when the idea was proposed.

And humble Heather was reluctant to participate at all, though she eventually came around to the idea when she thought about how her story could affect other people in similar positions.

Fast-forward several months. At an Airbnb in La Jolla, a beach town in Southern California, the three of us are seated around the kitchen table. It's been uncharacteristically wet and gray these past few days, but the serene view of the ocean from the porch is no worse for it. We've left our loved ones, jobs, and responsibilities to spend a week together: to reflect on how far we've come, and to identify the tools and resources that have helped us grow during these last several years.

None of us know how to "do grief right," and none of us believe there's only one right way to do it. We know how to do it wrong, though, because we've all erred at various points. We've lashed out at loved ones and checked out of daily life; we've drunk and self-medicated heavily, slept too much, and exercised and eaten too little. We've known anger and depression;

we've abandoned friendships and self-care. You name the tragic flaw or unhealthy coping mechanism, and we've all done it at one time or another.

But we've grown, too. We've found forgiveness, healing, and peace. We've realized just how much fight there is left in us, and how much opportunity has been afforded us.

We've challenged each other to embrace these moments of opportunity, and we fully expect to continue to learn. Our individual journeys don't all look the same, and they won't look like yours. But despite our differences, we have all learned one universal truth that applies to each of us:

Every human will struggle in this life. Our challenge is to struggle *well*.

Because after all, struggle is the antecedent of growth. It is only when we embrace the pain, heartache, and discomfort that punctuate our lives that we can ultimately find the strength we need to grow from those moments.

This is a fact of human existence, and it's as true at the molecular level as it is at the celestial one. Our muscles don't grow unless we literally damage our muscle fibers by exercising them strenuously. Only when those fibers have broken down can our body go through the natural process of repair and strengthening.

The same can be said for our planet. Earthquakes that rupture the earth's surface give birth to mountains.

Damage, breakdown, disruption—these are the prerequisites for growth. If this is true for the cells we're composed of, and it's true for the planet that supports us, then why shouldn't it be true for the lives we lead?

The notion that struggle leads to growth, and pain to strength, is widely accepted—in theory, anyway. The tricky part is translating this theory into practice. How do we live our daily lives in a way that embraces this philosophy? What is the best way to deal with the aftermath of a tragic knock at the door? Can we build enough resilience to prepare ourselves for the next knock?

We don't offer a manual to answer these questions for you. Instead we humbly submit a wealth of raw personal experiences from which we hope you will glean some insight. Some are ugly and some are beautiful, but they are all very real.

We challenge you to take the opportunity to reflect on the knock you've received at your own door, and to identify the areas in life where you can experience growth as a result. If you have the courage to love someone, to devote yourself to your craft, or to demonstrate passion, then—we promise—you, too, will receive a knock. Prepare yourself to open the door and greet whatever awaits. Because unfortunately in this life, opportunity isn't the only thing that comes knocking.

Ryan

★ ★ ★

★ ★ ★

CHAPTER 1

Sunday, April 29, 2007

I was in downtown Doylestown, Pennsylvania, scouting locations for a business I was opening. Doylestown is a quaint little suburb north of Philadelphia that evokes a different time. With a historic downtown brimming with shops and restaurants, it seemed like the perfect spot for a second location of my high-end women's and men's clothing store, Pale Moon Boutique.

Several years before, I had opened the first store in Avalon, New Jersey, a tiny resort town on a barrier island called Seven Mile Island. The business had been mostly seasonal, since Avalon was largely empty between

September and May. The store had become a labor of love for me, and I was thrilled to be selecting its newest location in the neighborhood where I'd grown up.

I had left my daughter, Maggie, with my parents while I and my business partner drove a few minutes away to look at a vacant store right in the heart of town. As soon as I saw it, I knew it would be perfect. As the landlord was putting the lease in my hand for me to sign, my cell phone rang, and I saw that it was my mom. Thinking she was just checking to see when I would be back, I ignored the call.

When my phone immediately rang again, I knew something was up. My initial fear was that something had happened to my ten-month-old daughter. My mind went to the worst place, and at the time, I didn't think anything could be worse than that.

When I answered the phone, all I heard on the other end were muffled screams. It was clearly a noise made by someone who was so broken up and in such a state of shock that he or she couldn't even cry properly. I didn't know how to prepare myself for whatever news I was about to receive.

I starting shaking uncontrollably. "Tell me what happened!" I cried. I was terrified that something horrible had happened to Maggie. Had she tripped and split her head open? Choked on something? My mind was running wild with the possibilities. Not knowing was almost worse than knowing at this point.

"Have you called an ambulance?" I yelled.

"Yes," answered the voice on the phone before the line suddenly went dead. The call had come from my mom's phone, but it wasn't until later that I learned that her sister, my aunt Annette, had been the caller. At the time, I had been too stunned to notice it wasn't my mom's voice on the other end. I knew that I was too upset to drive. I asked my business partner to take me home, a five-minute drive I had traveled countless times before. But this time, those five minutes felt like an eternity. And while the car was crawling through the streets, my mind was racing at a thousand miles a minute.

My husband was at work, about an hour away. While I wanted the comfort that his voice would bring, I decided not to call him until I got to the house and could figure out what was going on. I didn't want to upset him if I didn't have to.

As we pulled onto my parents' street, my heart started racing as fast as my mind. I didn't see an ambulance anywhere in sight. For a moment, that gave me a sense of relief. Maybe things weren't as serious as I had led myself to believe.

My dad was standing in the driveway next to a friend, Lieutenant Colonel Corky Gardner. He and my father had served together in the Marine Corps, and he was a dear friend of the family. He and his wife lived about forty-five minutes away, so it struck me as odd to see him standing there, especially since my parents had not mentioned he would be coming over.

I jumped out of the car while it was still moving.

"Where is the ambulance?" I screamed.

My dad stared at me with a blank look. Then in a very measured tone, he said, "Travis was killed."

I heard those words loud and clear, but they didn't make any sense to me. It took me a few seconds to process what I was being told. Since the moment I hung up the phone, I'd known something was wrong, but this was far worse than I could have imagined. I had thought my daughter was in imminent danger, and here I was being told that my brother was dead. He was twenty-six years old.

Travis and I had been born only fifteen months apart, so to say we were close would be an understatement. The fact that ours was a military family also brought us closer than most siblings. Like many military families, we'd had to adjust to new situations very quickly until I was twelve, when my dad left active duty. Before that, we had moved almost every two years.

We knew that, no matter where we moved next, no matter what school we ended up in or which sports teams we'd be the new kids on, we always had each other to depend on. Travis had been my built-in best friend at every stage of my life.

I couldn't believe it. I didn't want to believe it. I collapsed in a heap right there on the driveway. I remember thinking that the asphalt felt unnaturally warm for a mid-April afternoon that had been mild.

"It's not fair! It's not fair!" I screamed over and over into the sky. I wanted to make sure that everyone—even God himself—knew that he had made a terrible mistake. As I screamed, my parents' neighbors spilled out of their houses to find out what was happening.

My dad didn't rush to my side to comfort me. He let me get those tortured screams out of my system before I went about the hard work of trying to understand what had happened and pick up the pieces.

As had always been the case with my dad, he knew exactly what I needed before I did. I have no idea how long I lay on the ground screaming. I just know that it was long enough to get the rage out of my system. At some point, one of the neighbors helped me up and walked me down the driveway toward the house.

As I walked, I turned around and saw an unfamiliar car parked on the road in front of the house. In my shock, I hadn't even noticed it earlier.

Inside sat a young man, about my age, in full military dress blues. His forehead was resting on the top of the steering wheel, pressed between two folded arms that cradled his head. His eyes were closed and he looked dejected, or perhaps unconscious.

I later learned this poor Marine—twenty-six years old at most—had been charged with the unfortunate task of sharing the news with the people closest to

First Lieutenant Travis Manion that he had been killed in Iraq.

Captain Eric Cahill, as I later learned was his name, had been assigned to carry out the job since he was local and had graduated from the Naval Academy the year before my brother.

Lieutenant Colonel Gardner had also been called, since the military knew that he was a family friend close by. Together, while I had been out scouting sites for my boutique, they had approached my parents' door and knocked. My mother opened the door, took one look at Corky and the young Marine in uniform, and slammed the door in their faces.

She simply couldn't face what was on the other side.

I wasn't sure that I could, either. When I reached the front door with the help of my neighbor, I stopped. I had walked through that door thousands of times before, but this time I wanted to turn the other direction and run away. I knew, deep down in my soul, that once I passed through that door this time, the life that I had known was over and there was no going back.

Inside was pure pandemonium. My parents had been hosting a family barbecue when they received the knock at the door. Now, moments later, family members were scattered throughout the house, loudly sobbing, making hushed phone calls, and racing aimlessly back and forth.

I walked into a swarm of tumultuous and confused

activity, but my brain was still processing slowly. In all the chaos and furious movement, I locked eyes with my grandmother, who was seated alone in a wheelchair in the dining room, tears streaming down her cheeks. She was receiving neither comfort nor attention from anyone. My heart broke in that instant; I'll never forget that image.

The rest of that day is a blur. I floated between feelings of painful shock and dark emptiness. I finally emerged to a lucid state sometime later that night to inquire about my daughter's whereabouts. It had been hours since she even crossed my mind. Apparently, a friend had taken her from the house during the afternoon, and I hadn't even thought to ask until nightfall.

In the days that followed, it was as if I myself were a child. I couldn't care for my infant; I could barely care for myself. I lost ten pounds in seven days, from the day I learned of Travis's death to the day we held his funeral.

For a week, I slept between my parents in their bed. I found a bright-red Marine Corps sweatshirt in a forgotten drawer that had belonged to my father and I wore it religiously. As I sat on the back steps outside, it was in that sweatshirt. When I fell asleep at night, it was in that sweatshirt. And when I finally went to meet my brother's body upon arrival at Dover Air Force Base in Delaware, I carried the sweatshirt with me.

I hadn't planned to stay in Doylestown, of course.

I had planned to sign the lease to the new store and return that same day to my house in Avalon, a couple hours away.

That's where my clothing and the rest of my belongings were. So when I went to bed that first night, it was in that red sweatshirt and whatever I had worn all day. I remember being so grateful as I lay down in bed, looking forward to the moment when sleep would come over me and I could have a few hours of quiet forgetfulness, as though this terrible day had never happened.

When I woke the next morning, I remembered what it felt like coming out of anesthesia from an operation I'd had in college. First one eyelid opened cautiously, and then the next, but my body remained frozen. My mind was already churning, going over the details of the previous day and coming to terms with the unalterable fact that my best friend and brother was dead.

This marked the first of what turned out to be many anxiety-ridden mornings that would follow. Every day, I would slowly and warily transition from sleep to consciousness, hoping that my overwhelming anxiety wouldn't make another appearance. But it always did.

On one particular morning, I woke up thinking about the casket in which my brother would be arriving home that afternoon. What would it feel like to stand in the pouring rain in the middle of an airfield with my parents and my husband and watch the casket being carried solemnly off a military aircraft?

The house filled with another buzz of activity that morning as we all prepared to greet Travis and welcome him home. I stood in the kitchen with a few aunts and uncles, and one of them made a joke. What it was, I can't quite remember. I do remember knowing it was funny, but not being able to laugh. It simply wouldn't come. The rest of the group chuckled, grateful for a break from the heavy, somber mood of the previous few days. My uncle gently touched my arm and told me, "I promise you'll laugh again."

I really wanted to believe him. But I wasn't so sure.

The greeting at Dover was gut wrenching. My parents and I were plagued by questions in those early days that were difficult to ignore. Who was with Travis when he died? What happened? Was it instant? Slowly, the answers started to unfold.

We learned later that Travis wasn't actually scheduled to be out on the mission the day that he was killed. Instead, a fellow Marine was slated for the patrol, but he wasn't feeling up to it. Travis, who had been assigned to do some humanitarian work at a local Iraqi school, offered to take his place.

During the course of the patrol, Travis and his team of Marines were ambushed. A firefight erupted and they were quickly pinned down, taking fire from three sides. Travis, seeing his Navy corpsman shot and lying wounded in the middle of the road, immediately ran out into the line of fire to carry his colleague to safety.

As the ambush intensified, Travis again entered the line of fire to pull another wounded Marine back to safety in a covered position.

Then Travis moved out to take on the ambush that was now overwhelming his patrol. Undaunted by the onslaught, he fired his M203 grenade launcher, taking out an enemy position, and then expended a firestorm of rounds at the other positions before running out of ammunition. His efforts pushed the enemy back and changed the entire momentum of the ambush—ultimately saving the lives of his entire patrol.

It was then that Travis was shot by a sniper, and immediately the enemy began to pull back. His teammates quickly grabbed him and provided what emergency medical care they could. He was rushed back to Camp Fallujah, where he was pronounced dead by the medical staff that had worked feverishly to try and save him.

There's no part of that story that doesn't sound just like my brother. Offering to take the worse assignment to help a friend in need—that was Travis. Thinking about the safety of others before ever considering his own—that was Travis, too. Seeing dismal odds that didn't bode well for him and choosing to grit his teeth and answer fire with more fire anyway—also Travis. My brother was a protector and warrior in every sense of those terms. I certainly felt it as his sister, and I'm proud to know that his fellow Marines got to experience it, too.

When I learned that he'd been killed by a bullet,

I was nervous that I wouldn't be able to stomach the sight of him in an open casket. My mind imagined the worst. I was shocked, then, when the lid of the casket was raised at the viewing, to see my brother looking as though he were sleeping peacefully, just as I'd remembered him.

I approached the coffin and rubbed his head as I'd done a hundred times before. From the time he was a child, Travis had always sported a buzz cut, and as I felt the surface of his freshly cut hair with my fingertips, I thought, *Yep, that's Travis's head.*

I stood by his side all day, greeting friends and family who had taken the time to pay their respects. I was touched by visits from so many of Travis's friends, but there's one memory in particular that will always stay with me.

One of Travis's best friends and roommate at the Naval Academy, Brendan Looney, was unable to make the funeral. He was in San Diego attending the Basic Underwater Demolition/SEAL School (BUD/S), the training program required for Navy SEALs. Leaving to attend the services on the East Coast would have surely meant relinquishing his chance to become a SEAL officer.

But Brendan's girlfriend at the time, Amy, who had also been close to Travis, did come to say her final goodbye. I remember Amy walking up to the casket and bursting into tears. I knew that the loss cut her deeply as well.

The friends who traveled to see him lying in that casket were about his age. It felt terribly backward and wrong to see so many of them break down. For hours, I watched all these young, strong men, in the prime of their lives and in peak condition, weep at the sight of my brother, who appeared to be sleeping peacefully in front of them.

It was a physically and mentally exhausting day. And as much as I could hardly bear the idea of standing by that casket one minute longer after hours of doing so, I also didn't want to imagine that time coming to an end.

I knew that, after the last person knelt down to say a prayer in front of Travis, the funeral director was going to close that casket forever, and that would be it. I'd never see my brother's face again. I rubbed his head one last time and felt my heart sinking as my father gently pulled me away.

There hadn't been much discussion around where to bury Travis. Before he left, he had tried to talk with me about it. We were having a couple of beers and he casually mentioned that, if anything were to happen to him, he would want to be buried at Arlington. I abruptly ended the conversation, telling him we were not having that discussion and steering the conversation in another direction.

My mom wanted Travis to be interred in the family plot in Pennsylvania so that she could visit him regularly; I refrained from telling her what Travis had told me.

After the funeral, the burial, and the celebration of his life that followed, I remember sitting on the back stairs outside my parents' home, the same place where I had sought solace in the chaos after first hearing of his death. The winter had melted away and a beautiful spring day had sprung up in its place. I sat, arms wrapped around my knees, enveloped by the big, red Marine Corps sweatshirt. I stared into the pond behind my parents' home and noticed a large goose waddling into the water from the grass. Then I noticed she was being trailed by half a dozen baby geese. It was strange to see these lively, innocent, and sweet creatures in spring juxtaposed against the backdrop of my own feelings, gray and bleak.

In the weeks and months that followed, I often found myself outside, crouched on a stair in that same position, searching for my little family of geese and wondering what the day had in store for them. Then one day, as I sat there, I saw them all fly away.

It sounds silly to say this now, but watching them disappear into the sky left me with such an empty feeling. All of the sadness that had been flowing through me during the previous weeks hardened into a solid knot that dropped like a rock into the pit of my stomach.

Time was passing. Life was moving on. I was watching it happen, but I was not participating in it. I felt bitterness toward the people who could return to their normal lives, jobs, and families, while I sat on the same stair, in the same red sweatshirt, terrified of what might come next.

It was hard to believe that, only weeks before, I had been so happy, blissfully ignorant of how my life would be cruelly, abruptly, and permanently changed. I remember sitting in my kitchen two weeks before Travis died. I was watching my baby girl, all of nine and a half months old, pull herself up to stand. On uncertain and wobbly legs, she stood with her chubby hands on the screen of the door; she stood next to our dog Pup and giggled excitedly as she peered outside and watched a bunny rabbit hop around the backyard.

Life is so completely perfect, I remember thinking at that moment. I was a happy new mom. I had a fantastic relationship with my husband. Business was good, and Travis would be back in time for the grand opening of my second store. I felt wholly in control and at peace.

To this day, that peaceful feeling sometimes comes back to me for a moment—when life feels effortless, my mind is at ease, and all seems right in the world.

But now it dissolves in an instant. In fact, as soon as I experience that kind of serenity, I become terrified. *What terrible tragedy is going to shatter this picture of peace?* I ask myself. I still wonder if the sense of calm I experienced that day had been a harbinger of the doom to come. I worry that I was foolish not to have recognized it for what it was. All the signs of catastrophe were right in front me. How could I have been so blind?

This train of thought is, of course, completely para-noid and insane. It's a shame that pain can become so deeply pressed into our past that it robs us of the joys of our future. And though I recognize the thought process as irrational, I also know that it's just one of the many profound ways that my brother's sudden death has changed me.

I'm not naive enough to believe that, because some devastating tragedy struck my family once, it won't strike again. It's almost as though I look for it now.

I used to watch those horrific news stories on NBC's *Dateline* with a distant fascination. Now, if I watch them at all, it's because I want to know *exactly* what dangers are out there so I can prepare myself and my family for them. A ten-year-old girl walks out the door to take the garbage out and never returns home; a young mother disappears only to be found dead on the side of a country road; I simply can't absorb these kinds of stories casually anymore.

The fear and paranoia that follow in the wake of grief can create a tremendous roadblock. It stunts our personal growth and darkens our overall sense of well-being. Some people respond to unexpected and trying situations with passive acquiescence, and others with fire and fury. I responded by heightening my vigilance. After Travis's death, I found myself compelled to be wary. I was always on the lookout for the next great tragedy to befall me.

This hurled me down some very dark and troublesome paths, from panic attacks to self-destructive behaviors. But it also led me to some amazing gifts, like recovering my sense of humor and living with intention.

My brother's death has changed me in many ways, some for the worse, some for the better. I'm not proud to admit that, before Travis died, I had developed a mild callousness about the suffering of others and skepticism about the possibility that I myself might experience a similar fate.

I remember being wrapped up in my own little world in college, for instance, when my dad called to tell me that my grandfather had died. He told me when the funeral services would be held and I immediately shot back: "Dad, I'm sorry but I can't go. I've got finals."

It's crazy to me now that I responded that way. Was I really going to miss such a salient moment for exams? Did I even consider the sadness that my dad was feeling? No, I didn't. Even when Travis deployed, for the first *and* second times, I don't think I fully appreciated the gravity of the moment or the support I should have given.

It was 2006 and 2007. Yes, I was vaguely aware that service members were dying, but I rarely thought about them. They weren't Travis. My brother was one of thousands of highly trained warriors doing this job. And he was great at it. Everyone who knew Travis reinforced that to me whenever we talked about his deployment. What were the chances that something would go wrong?

It's an ugly thought, I know. And an uncomfortable one to dredge back up. Unfortunately, it's one of many memories I have that make me cringe. There were many times where I managed my grief poorly, particularly in the earliest days after we received the knock at the door. In one instance, only days after Travis was killed, I saw red and completely tore into a stranger whom I felt was disrespecting my brother's sacrifice.

There was a civic building in our town that, as a political statement, tallied the deaths of all the men and women killed in the war on terror. Travis was familiar with the building, and had criticized the display as distasteful. One day, before his deployment, he entered the building and told the people responsible for the display that he found it disgraceful. They responded that they thought it was important that the public know young men and women were dying.

"If you really care," Travis told them, "put their names up there. Let people learn their names and remember them."

A couple days after his death, I noticed that the number on the front of the building had increased by one. I stormed into the office and ripped apart some poor employee at the front desk.

"Don't you dare change that number for my brother!"
I screamed at her. "He's not just a f*cking number!"

Yikes.

As I write this more than a decade later, I feel very
disconnected from the woman who stormed into that
office. What was I thinking?

But that's what an unexpected and unwelcome knock
at the door can do to you. The fact is, grief *will*
transform you. Whether you are grieving the loss of an
identity you once had or the loss of a loved one, at
some point, you will look in the mirror and see someone you simply don't recognize staring back at you. It's
inevitable. Maybe you'll be proud of what you see, and
maybe you'll be ashamed. At some point, I'd bet, you'll
be both.

The most important thing you can tell yourself is that
you get the last word. Only you can determine how your
experiences will change you. And only you can be held
accountable for that transformation.

The experiences of April 29, 2007, ignited a chain of
events that at different times has left me feeling hopeless, infuriated, and destructive. Through the years,
I've bounced from convictions of strength and control
to unexpected bouts of powerlessness and despair.

Like anyone who has received a jarring knock at
the door—literal or figurative—I've been to the darkest, deepest, and ugliest corners of my mind. And I've
learned a thing or two. I don't hope to spare you the

hurt or pain that comes with that knock. I don't think I could. I only hope to share the lessons I learned in the process: the ones that have the power to transform you—in all the right ways—and to remind you that you are not alone.

★ ★ ★

A Few Months Out:
My Drug of Choice

On a wooden beam in our basement, by the bench press on which he would punish himself nightly, Travis wrote his goals in permanent black marker.

All-American Wrestler
1st Team All Catholic in Lacrosse
Maintain 3.9 GPA

My aspirations were far more modest, rarely re-corded, and—let's be honest—not terribly admirable. While Travis's key performance indicators consisted of grade point averages and athletic milestones, mine were quantified by number of parties attended or classes skipped without getting caught. Travis had a work ethic uncommon among most sixteen-year-olds, and as his older sister I found it fascinating, and a little unnerving. I marveled at Travis's ability to set a goal one year out— even two years—and then work tirelessly to meet it.

Occasionally, I questioned what genetic material was absent from my DNA that caused this quality to skip me, but I never lost sleep about it. And though I admired his self-discipline and focus, I'm pretty sure Travis envied my vibrant social life and lighthearted attitude toward responsibility.

In the finished section of that same basement, Travis and I would spend every Friday and Saturday night. No matter what may have been on our individual agendas for the night, we always ended up at our usual rendezvous spot: making sandwiches; chatting about our friends and complaining about our enemies; arguing over who got control of the TV remote; and, ultimately, falling asleep on adjacent couches.

During one such weekend, I told him about a party that was scheduled for the following Saturday night. An upperclassman's parents would be out of town, and the entire school was already abuzz over how many kegs would be delivered to the house and who was going to be there. "You should come, Trav," I said. Referring to my best friend, I added, "You can drive Krista and me."

Travis was in the throes of wrestling season at La Salle

College High School, an all-boys Catholic institution outside Philadelphia.

As a freshman, I had attended its sister school, Gwynedd Mercy Academy, after my parents pleaded with me to give it a shot. As soon as the year was over, I returned to public school, having never really given myself the chance to like the parochial school.

Given his goals, Travis was not a big partier, but he was sociable, well liked, and needed a change of scenery, so I thought my party invitation wasn't a half-bad idea.

The following weekend, Travis and I pulled into Krista's driveway and he beeped the horn. I was thrilled to have my little brother as chauffeur for the evening and made him pick up several other friends from their houses before we all headed over to the north side of town for the party.

A few hours into the festivities, the cops arrived, lights flashing, and we teenagers scattered like cockroaches. Travis, Krista, and I quickly found one another and joined the mad rush toward the back of the house. We barreled through the kitchen door, hopped the fence that surrounded the property, and sprinted for the woods behind the house.

Those woods were our ticket to freedom. They also represented a blessed escape from the terrifying wrath of my parents, who almost certainly would have disowned me for what would have been the *third* underage drinking citation in my high school career.

As we kids charged across a small footbridge at the back of the property, I got thrown and ended up in a shallow creek a few feet below.

Travis quickly scooped me up onto dry land and we continued our sprint until the terrain opened into a vast cornfield and we knew we were safe. I stopped and took a deep breath. Standing still for that moment, as the moonlight poured over us, I became aware of pain coursing through my leg. I looked down and saw that my shin was covered in blood. My khaki pants were red.

"We gotta go back," Travis said, observing my leg. "We have to take care of that."

Hell no, I thought. Did I mention this would be my third underage? I had too much on the line. If I was going out, I was going out in this cornfield, with my two best friends, not into the hands of furious parents. Krista pleaded with me to stop being so stubborn.

Travis was calm but stern. He had made up his mind. We were going back and that was it. He was right, of course, as he usually was, and he persuaded me to turn back. He hadn't been drinking, and if he could just get us to where the car was parked, we'd quietly slip in and drive away—no problem.

Krista hung back with other friends as they moved deeper into the cornfield to wait out the police. No sense in her getting caught, too. As Travis and I started to trek back, I felt the mixture of blood and creek water sloshing around in my shoes, and with each step a piercing, throbbing sensation cutting through my leg. Finally, we closed in on the property and the car was within sight.

But just as we rounded a giant pine tree, a blinding light shone in our eyes.

Busted.

"Hey! Kids! Get over here." A square-jawed officer examined us with his flashlight. He wanted names, ages, and a full account of our whereabouts that evening. Somewhere in the interrogation session, a lightbulb seemed to go off in his head. His eyes softened and his lips turned up into a smile. "Hey, wait. You're Travis Manion, you said?"

"Yes, sir."

"Hell of a wrestling season you're having, kid."

"Thank you, sir."

Travis was no fool. He saw an opportunity and he seized it. The two of them chatted like old friends: semifinals, school records, weight classes, and who would be best positioned to take on that heavyweight monster from Archbishop Wood High School next weekend. That kid was huge. Were we even sure he was a teenager? I stood nervously behind him trying to play the part of the cool, calm, and collected older sister who hadn't just drunk a six-pack of Sierra Nevada Pale Ale and wasn't hiding a pretty significant injury.

Within minutes, the police officer was chuckling and giving Travis a pretend right hook to the shoulder.

Two more minutes of polite charm and verbal jujitsu and Travis artfully changed the subject. "Sir, this is my sister, Ryan, and her leg is bleeding pretty badly. I haven't been drinking tonight, and I'd like to get her to a hospital. I think she needs stitches, sir."

The police officer suddenly seemed to remember he was busting high school kids at a keg party and not catching up with an old friend. For the first time, he turned his attention toward me and looked disapprovingly at my leg. He glanced side-to-side quickly and turned back to grimace at us. "Get outta here," he commanded. "Now!" He didn't need to tell us twice.

Once inside the car, with Travis behind the steering wheel, we looked at each other.

"I can't go to the hospital," I pleaded, my voice higher-pitched than I expected.

"Yeah, no kidding," Travis said. "Mom and Dad will kill us if they find out."

I didn't, in fact, get the stitches I needed that night, and I've got a pretty nasty scar to prove it. But thanks to Travis, I didn't get the underage drinking citation, either. What I did get was a lesson in pain management that I've had to learn over and over again since my brother's death: Adrenaline is one hell of a drug.

When fear hits, your pulse spikes, your legs start moving before you even tell them to, and you don't feel a thing. It's amazing. You're speeding to the next target: the back door, the footbridge, the woods. You're almost home free. Is your leg bleeding? Who knows? Who cares? You're moving with wild abandon and an eye on the next marker.

That is, until you're not. Eventually, the moonlight shines down to expose the truth, and pretty soon you're not moving at all.

This was my experience with grief after losing my brother. At first, I couldn't imagine putting on a fresh pair of pants in the morning or forcing down a little bit of breakfast. But once I got past those first few zombie-like days of merely surviving, my brain went into hyperdrive.

It wanted to make up for all that lost time when it had nearly wilted away. Pretty soon, the thoughts were flowing like water from a fire hose: What do they mean, a sniper shot him? Are they sure he's dead? Was he in pain? Was he alone? What about my daughter? How will she ever get to know her uncle Travis? What about me? What about the memories we still had left to make?

Fear and sadness and anxiety would creep from my brain to my spine, and in that moment I'd give anything to quiet the inner monologue that was quickly taking over. I needed a goal. I needed focus. I needed a distraction. I needed to keep moving. I couldn't risk pausing long enough for my brain to remember what was going on. Just keep sprinting for the cornfield. Don't let the moon shine down and remind you of the wound.

As I said, adrenaline is a powerful drug. But it's not

always a bad one. In fact, it's gotten me through some of the darkest days of my life. It's my drug of choice.

Having an immediate goal to work toward and enough shock in the system to fuel it can be an incredibly potent antidote to grief. I would hungrily swallow up any invitation that promised to pull me out of the darkness or distract me from the black, heavy cloud over my head. Anything to force me out of bed in the morning and channel my focus to a simple task in front of me.

Many reasonable people whose worlds have been rocked by tragedy choose to work toward well-measured, appropriate goals. Such goals provide them with a structure that fills otherwise empty days and gives meaning to lives that otherwise may appear empty.

Without them, these people might fall apart. But with them, they can make progress—slow, steady, and encouraging progress. Growth happens in stages.

That's not how I typically do things. Or I should say, it's not how I'm hardwired to do things.

In the early days after Travis was killed, my decision making was more impulsive than rational. Impulsive decisions can be catastrophic, and a few of mine have been. But they've also been a great way for me to channel my nervous energy.

I think, subconsciously, I believed that as long as I was doing something—anything—then I wouldn't have to acknowledge the intense pain that was overtaking my spirit and fighting to get out. It's sort of like when your leg is bleeding out in a stampede of intoxicated teenagers through the woods, but you're too hopped up on a cocktail of fear and motion to notice—if you catch my drift.

People have told me I'm courageous and I'd like to think that I am. But it's not always courage that spurs me on. Sometimes it's pure bullheadedness. Rather than testing the waters by slowly working my way into the shallow end of the pool, I tend to catapult myself off the diving board into the deep end, where I hit the water in a graceless, but powerful cannonball.

But what happens if you don't know how to swim?

Ignorance can make you fearless and bold; it can also force you to learn some critical survivor skills on the fly. For better or for worse, embracing my own ignorance in the spirit of boldness proved to be one of the ways I channeled my grief after my brother died.

Two weeks before he was killed, Travis called home from Iraq. "I want to run the Marine Corps Marathon," he told my dad.

"That's great, Trav," my dad responded.

"And I want you to run it with me," he finished.

My father was then in his early fifties and in solid shape, but this was no small request. After running the Marine Corps Marathon a couple of times when he was younger, my dad had retired his marathon shoes— forever, he thought. But he wasn't about to say no to his son fighting a war thousands of miles away.

"Let's do it," he replied.

In mid-May, when the funeral services were over and my parents, extended family, and friends were gathered in the living room, my dad remembered his promise to Travis. "I'm still going to run that marathon," he proclaimed to the quiet gathering of distraught, dumbstruck family members.

"I'll run too, Tom," said Chris, my dad's youngest brother.

"I'm in," echoed his wife, my aunt Susan.

One by one, people picked up their heads, hardened their gazes, and joined him. Pretty soon, every single person in that room had committed to 26.2 miles in honor of Travis. I was conveniently engrossed in a thread in the carpet when I felt a dozen pairs of eyes landing intently on my face. I looked up.

Now, I had been an athlete in college, but that was almost five years earlier. I had given birth to Maggie only ten months before and I hadn't run so much as a 5K in ages. But those stares were burning a hole right through my skin, and thankfully my bullheadedness kicked in.

"All right, I'll do it," I said. I mean, how hard it could it be?

On June 1, a couple of weeks later, training began. I was in Avalon, whose flat roads, wide sidewalks, and ocean views would make training runs a breeze. It was a beginner's paradise. I printed out my couch-to-marathon training plan and set out on my first run—one mile. That was it.

Things started to go south immediately. My heart felt like it might explode, and every breath in was a sharp stab in my side. I finished that mile, but it wasn't pretty. How was I going to run 25.2 more of those by the last week of October?

I had underestimated the effort that would be required for me to reach my goal. Or maybe I had overestimated myself. Either way, I didn't dwell on it. I couldn't allow my mind to wander down any path that might end in surrender.

At the end of that first run, wheezing forcefully and doubled over in pain, I gave myself a little pat on the back. *Good job, Ryan. You did today's run. You're done now. Go home, drink some water, and chill. But make damn sure you show up for tomorrow's run.*

And that's how it went. Every day for four and a half months. No matter how slow, ugly, or painful the run may have been, I completed it. There was no 26.2-mile run ahead of me. There was only today.

As the proverb says, "There's only one way to eat an elephant: one bite at a time."

At the time, I believed that the Marine Corps Marathon was my elephant, and every training run a nibble. I know now that that goal actually meant something much bigger. It wasn't simply physical and mental preparation for an athletic feat. It meant honoring my brother's sacrifice. It meant committing to his memory and to my family to be a better version of myself tomorrow than I was today. It meant doing something tough and challenging, and choosing a healthier outlet for all the fear and outrage and sadness that was churning inside me like a tornado.

The big, gaping hole that Travis's death had left in my heart was yet another elephant, sitting square on my chest. And every day, one mile at a time, I took a little nip out of those elephants and thereby lessened the pain.

Perhaps the greatest help I got in completing that summer's training was the discovery of Travis's iPod, which kept me company on my long runs. It had been shipped back from Iraq along with his other personal effects—letters, photos, magazines. Every morning I'd wake up, tie my shoelaces, pop in my earbuds, and think to myself, *All right, DJ Travis, what do you have for me today?*

I'd be running along the water and smile to myself when Crosby, Stills, Nash & Young would come on and I'd remember the time Travis and I heard them in concert in Philadelphia. Then Jewel would belt out "Who Will Save Your Soul" and jolt me out of my sweet little daydream. *Of course,* I thought. I chuckled when I remembered what an enormous crush Travis had on Jewel growing up.

Training for that marathon proved to be the most

disciplined effort I'd ever undertaken. It was exactly the challenge and distraction I needed. A lot of hard work, a strong commitment to my family, and an eclectic iPod playlist were all I needed that summer. I suffered a pretty good tweak to my left knee with a small tear in my meniscus on my final long run—eighteen miles— but I still felt ready to take on the Marine Corps Marathon that October.

As the big date approached, my family and I headed to Washington, through which the marathon course runs. The night before the race, we held a dinner for our team—which by now had grown to nearly a hundred people: aunts, uncles, cousins, friends, neighbors, lacrosse and wrestling buddies, fellow Marines and Naval Academy grads. All of them were participating to honor my brother.

At dinner at a hotel, we invited a few people, including Brendan Looney, to say a few words. Brendan stood solemnly at the microphone. He started in about how Travis had been a brother to him and how he couldn't believe he was gone.

"He was a great friend," Brendan said. "I'll never forget him, and I miss him."

He had been choking back tears, and his voice finally broke.

I have to get out of this room, I thought. I simply couldn't watch this tough Navy SEAL break down as he remembered my brother. It was too much.

I slipped out of the hotel and found myself gulping in the cold fall night air outside. My head was spinning and I couldn't help but feel that I was learning for the first time that Travis was gone forever.

I lit a cigarette. It had been an on-and-off habit of mine over the years, one that Travis always chastised me about. I can't tell you how long I stood outside, inhaling deeply and focusing on nothing but blowing the smoke out of my lungs. I might have been halfway through my first cigarette or I might have been well into my fifth. But eventually, a gentle hand touched my arm.

"I know this is a lot. And I'm sure you're nervous," a voice said. I turned around to see my uncle Chris, who was also my godfather and had been one of Travis's mentors. He calmly asked—in a way that only my uncle Chris could—"Do you think a cigarette is a good idea before a twenty-six-mile run?" We both burst out laughing at the sheer ridiculousness of the question.

Through the years, I have seen many friends and colleagues challenge themselves to run a marathon. One of the things I feared most about making that commitment is that I would not be prepared.

I see that same fear in others, too. I love to talk to people leading up to the race as they tell me they are not sure if they are eating enough protein or they don't know how their failure to complete a few of the runs laid out in their plans will affect their performance. It is then that I like to share with them that nothing could be worse than smoking cigs less than twelve hours before the starting gun. I tell them that, if I could do that and still complete my marathon, they will more than likely be just fine. This typically calms their nerves, since most people can't comprehend someone being stupid enough to do what I did.

Maybe one day I'll write a book about what *not* to do when marathon training. Chain smoking the night before the race would certainly make the list, but it's not even the worst transgression I've committed. Fortunately for you, this isn't a book about endurance training. It's a book about grief, which perhaps isn't so different. *The key to navigating grief, I've found, is to have the courage to allow it to transform you.*

I imagine there are plenty of seasoned professionals, renowned therapists, and successful counselors who will insist I shouldn't be advising on that, either. Maybe they're right. Committing to a twenty-six-mile run and a brand-new lifestyle within weeks of a loved one's death may not be a good idea. Neither is inhaling cigarette smoke before you take on the greatest physical challenge of your life.

But as I've had to remind myself time and time again, we're only human. We can take only so much. Don't be so hard on yourself when you take one step forward and several steps back. You made it this far. You got up today and put one foot in front of the other. You completed today's run. Go home, relax. Get ready for tomorrow's.

When I left that night, I was a complete mess. But when I woke up the next morning, I was a new woman. I was going to crush this run and I was not going to do it alone. I knew that, along with my aunt Susan, who had committed to running with me, Travis was going to trot effortlessly alongside me as we jammed to a mix of Creedence Clearwater Revival and Eminem. The mental image of Travis pushing me along carried me through the first eighteen miles. I was sailing. More than once, I even caught myself thinking how easy the run was.

Until I hit the base of the bridge.

I was making my way into Crystal City, Virginia, and had reached the critical point in the run that determines whether you get to finish—or not. Right around mile eighteen, a bus comes and scoops up the slow-moving stragglers so race officials can begin to reopen the roads to traffic.

All of my training leading up to race day had been about beating that bus to the bridge. As long as I made it over the bridge, I could walk the rest of the way. It seemed easy enough in my head. What I didn't factor in was that, once I beat the bridge and got to mile 19, I still had 7.2 miles to complete.

At this point, the wheels had all but come off. My brain was no longer able to bully my body into behaving. My knees, my ankles, my arches—everything was rebelling. I had slowed to a walk and began a debate with myself that any distance runner knows well:

Eighteen miles is great. You should be proud of yourself. There's no shame in stopping here. You just lost your brother, for God's sake. Did anyone really expect you to get this far? Call it now and leave with your dignity and joints intact.

It was a compelling argument, and my broken-down body had nothing to offer as a rebuttal. I could almost hear those plush bus seats calling for me.

My aunt Susan remained a positive force, telling me that we were almost done and urging me to keep going. But even her words sounded hollow. I needed to get in a different headspace.

I made one last-ditch effort. I reached into my fanny pack and rifled through my unused power gels and energy beans until my fingers rested on the Mass card with Travis's face on it. November 19, 1980–April 29, 2007. Twenty-six years old. I gripped it tightly and offered a silent prayer. *This is it, Travis. You better freaking do something* this minute *or I'm letting that bus pick us up.*

The knee I had tweaked during my last training run was throbbing so forcefully that I could have sworn it had a heartbeat. I looked down just to make sure. I surveyed my left leg, and my eyes fell on the scar from that night so many years before. It was a nice reminder. Travis always came through when I needed him.

Funny, I thought. That night he saved me by *giving*

me a ride, and now I needed him to prevent me from *getting* one. The irony was enough to set my legs back in motion, ever so slowly.

I started taking the bridge and, right at the crest, I saw my best friend, Krista, in the crowd. She was holding a sign and screaming like a madwoman alongside Lia, another of my best friends from high school. They later told me that I looked like a battered and bruised Frankenstein dragging my limp left leg behind me.

At the time, thankfully, I was so out of touch with my body—and reality—that I didn't care. Their cheers echoed in my ears and carried me all the way to mile twenty-four, where I received another well-timed show of support. Uncle Chris, who had finished the race nearly two hours earlier, had come back for me and Susan. He met us just two miles short of the finish line and we pushed through those last minutes silently, but together. About a hundred yards before the finish line, we came upon the final hill. At that point, it might as well have been Mount Everest. *Am I going to be able to scale this thing?* I asked myself.

The Marine Corps Marathon course ends at the US Marine Corps War Memorial, a statue based on the iconic picture of six Marines struggling to raise a flagpole on the island of Iwo Jima during World War II.

It's an incredibly powerful sight, and when you come upon it, you feel every bit as tired and as strong as those men huddled together appear to be as they raise the

American flag. I didn't care if my leg fell off in that very moment. I was *not* walking up that hill.

I hustled into a full sprint, bounded over crushed plastic cups, and passed exhausted runners. Somehow I felt that my legs were fresh. In reality, I was probably every bit the Frankenstein I had appeared to be at mile nineteen, just an hour older.

What I actually looked like, I can't say for sure. And I'd rather not imagine. But I pushed forward and grabbed Aunt Susan's hand as, together, we crossed the finish line.

Then I collapsed.

I could not make it another step. Uncle Chris pulled me up and onto his back. He piggybacked me to the water station, to refreshments, to the meet-up spot where the rest of the team had gathered, and all the way to the metro station. I remember thinking, *Holy crap, I actually finished!* And I ignored the physical pain that was pulsing through my body.

I can honestly say that I'm a different person because of that race. Pushing myself through that training and navigating the emotional strain and physical stress taught me a lot about myself and even more about grief.

It took me years to process my brother's death, and years more to organize my thoughts around what wisdom I could possibly gain from it. It's only after more than a decade of reflection that I can share what I now know.

FIRST, WHAT YOU DON'T KNOW CAN'T HURT YOU.

Wait. Hear me out. I know this advice is usually given sarcastically, and that can be for good reason. But consider, for a moment, the wisdom in that phrase. Sometimes, naïveté is a blessing. If I had known the physical, mental, or emotional toll that the race would take on me, I wouldn't have run it. I would have become paralyzed by fear and self-doubt, and my eyes would have remained forever fixed on that thread in the carpet.

But fear and self-doubt often keep us from knowing our own strength. And that's something we simply can't risk. If I had never run that race, I would never have discovered what I was capable of achieving. Sometimes the best way to learn how to swim is to spring from the diving board and cannonball into the deep end of the pool.

And a wet, cold shock to the system may prove to be the only thing that can wake you from a heavy bout of grief, reclusiveness, or apathy. Don't get me wrong: There's value in preparation. Without the structure of that couch-to-marathon training plan, and the luxury of months to train, I never would have made it.

Preparation and training are great tools; they provide us with the confidence to dream as big as we want to. But without a healthy dose of fearless ignorance, we might never bother dreaming at all.

SECOND, EMBRACE YOUR SUPPORT SYSTEM.

Relationships are *everything*. Family, friends, and loved ones can get us through our darkest and saddest moments. We just need to let them. Our friends and families feed our wild ambitions and nourish our ill-conceived dreams. When we share with them some embarrassing fantasy that's well beyond our reach, they say, "Go for it." And if you're lucky enough to have a family and friends like mine, they may even say, "I'm in. Let's do it together."

They gently and lovingly protect us from our own self-destructive habits. They lift us up (literally) when we can't go another step, and they cheer us on when we look like Frankenstein. With a loving support system, we can afford to be a little naive. Be bold. Be fearless. But don't do it alone. You are human and you are one person. Allow yourself to be carried forward by those who love you.

AND FINALLY, DON'T WAIT.

I beg you, please don't wait. I had no idea how tough I was. Why did I wait until my brother was dead to find out? My only regret of that marathon in 2007 was that it didn't take place in 2006. You know who would have loved to run and train with me? Travis. Something like that, which required focus and discipline, was far more up his alley than mine. He would have been so proud and we would have had a ball together. There are so many things I wish we could have done together. I'm not the same woman he knew when he was alive. I'm better. I'm stronger. Why did I wait for him to disappear before I became the woman I wanted to be?

CHAPTER 3

★ ★ ★

A Few Years Out:
A Lesson in Restraint

Throwing myself into an arduous task that required long-term focus and discipline—and for which I was largely unprepared—proved to be a blessing for me.

The steroid shot I had received in my knee only weeks before that marathon was a strong indicator that my body wasn't up to the task. The hours-long adventure through Washington on my uncle Chris's back afterward was confirmation.

After I finished that race, I was completely debilitated. And although I have zero regrets about the way I achieved my goal, the health professionals reading this book can breathe a sigh of relief knowing I don't recommend that anyone treat their body the way I did mine in October 2007.

I wish I could say that was the last time I made an impulsive decision that landed me in way over my head, but it wasn't. Not even close. My gut has a habit of seizing opportunities and committing to goals that my brain could never dream up and that my body can only barely support. It has been a pattern for me over the years. And as with all patterns, it ends the same way. It buys me some time, and a respite from my overwhelming grief.

But sooner or later, I have to pay for it. In the case of the marathon, I was paying for it the following day, when every cell in my body hurt and I had to relearn how to walk. But that was nothing in comparison with the emotional toll the whole process had taken—and would continue to take.

If you've run a marathon—or achieved any other hard-fought goal—you know that special high that the accomplishment brings with it. Nothing tastes so sweet as the fruits of your own labor. When you land the job you've been relentlessly pursuing, or finally save enough money to buy that car you've been eyeing, you feel certain that nothing compares to that first taste of victory.

You show up for your first day at your new position or slide behind the wheel for that very first time, and you think life can't get any better. And what happens a week later, or maybe a month, without fail? That's right, you forget. The joy, the feeling of achievement, that you once got from the thing—the job, the car— disappears, and life goes back to normal. You're going to need something else to pursue if you want to feel that high again. The first lick of an ice cream cone is always the best, isn't it? The fifteenth just can't compare.

I've heard this concept, this inevitable part of human nature, referred to as "the hedonic treadmill." *Hedonism* is the pursuit of pleasure, so you can imagine what the inventors of that term were getting at when they intro- duced the image of a treadmill. We fervently chase the thing that will bring us happiness. A title, a relation- ship, a feeling. And if we're lucky, we actually capture it. It feels just as great—maybe even greater—than we imagined. Wonderful.

But humans are nothing if not adaptable. Our ability to adapt has ensured our survival on this planet. So like the good *Homo sapiens* that we are, we adapt to that feeling of joy. What was once pleasure and gratification is now just another day. And we search for our next high.

If this sounds like the pattern of an addict, that's because it is. On some level, we are all addicts. We're all chasing the things that feel good to us—love, a sense of belonging, connectedness, purpose, achievement. And they're inherently good things. It's normal and good that we would want more of them in our lives. And we find these things in different places, of course.

I found mine at the Marine Corps Marathon of 2007.

If you were to graph my emotions for that year, you would produce an interesting line: a fairly stable, horizontal line of "contentment" for the beginning of the year; a drastic drop in April, when Travis died; then a gradual climb back upward toward happiness until the marathon, six months later.

I was so grateful to have something to focus on that helped me put the pieces of my life back together after the loss of my brother. It was precisely the medicine I needed, and I wouldn't trade that experience for anything. But by winter, my line was dropping again. The decline in my happiness and well-being was persistent, steady, and, interestingly, almost undetectable.

I, of course, knew my life had been far better when Travis was in it, but I was managing, wasn't I? After all, I was getting up, going to work, being a mom. I was running errands and knocking out personal goals. I was socializing and even laughing and finding joy here and there. By any external barometer, I was improving. I was wounded, no doubt, but I was happy.

But grief is very much an internal battle. It's not kind enough to play by the rules, and it certainly doesn't register on any emotional barometer. It can be deceptive. And believe it or not, so can you. In fact, I would wager that no one can deceive you as effectively as you can deceive yourself.

We are able to survive only because we are able to adapt, right?

Grief, pain, sadness—these feel like disadvantages. They threaten our survival, so naturally we shed them. We convince ourselves that they've gone away. This is precisely what I did. And it's amazing what I managed to hide from myself, and for how long.

My emotional slope continued to creep stealthily downward. For several years. It continued right under my nose until Christmas night of 2012, when I reached rock bottom. But the seeds of my deterioration had been planted several years before.

December 25 is the date reserved for the annual Manion Family Christmas Party. This party dates back to when my father was a child. As a young man, my father's father started the tradition, and every year since, it has been a sight to behold.

After my grandfather stopped hosting the party, my great-uncle Nick and my great-aunt Marilyn organized the festivities. Then shortly after I graduated from college, my parents began hosting the event.

It was a big deal. No less than one hundred of our closest family, friends, and neighbors would gather at my parents' home in Doylestown, Pennsylvania. For a few hours, pandemonium reigned. There were teenagers coasting down banisters, children erupting into spontaneous games of tag between rooms, tipsy aunts and uncles sharing old stories with each other, and enough food, dips, cookies, and pies to keep us all busy for hours.

At a certain point in the evening, right when we couldn't decide if the warmth in our bones was from the crackling fireplace or the third glass of wine, Mitch Miller's rendition of "Must Be Santa" would blast through the speakers and one of my uncles, dressed as Santa Claus, would come down the stairs carrying a sack full of presents he had "forgotten" to deliver the night before.

I remember, as a child, being the envy of all my friends when I would share with them that Santa came to my house every year on Christmas night. Even today, as this tradition continues, I love nothing more than watching the joy in the eyes of my children and young cousins.

This tradition was a staple, and it simply wouldn't have felt like Christmas without it. But for one year in particular, 2006, it almost didn't feel like Christmas *with* it. That was the year we learned that Travis would be deployed for a second time to Iraq. He would be leaving on December 26 from his base at Camp Pendleton in San Diego.

It felt almost sacrilegious to host a party with all our loved ones that Travis couldn't attend. He had come home a few weeks earlier but returned to the West Coast just a couple of days before Christmas. I was grateful to have had that time with him, but I still felt upset that he was going to miss this year's party. My feelings toward the holiday party had become more bitter than sweet. My mom, however, wasn't having it.

"Of course we're having the party this year," she told me when I voiced my concern.

As with most things, she was unwavering, emphatic, and insistent. She got to work preparing dishes, making shopping trips, and cleaning the house for the party. In addition to our usual tree that year, she went out and bought a smaller, artificial tree and covered it with mementos of Travis: Marine Corps and patriotic ornaments, little photos, and red, white, and blue decorations. She wanted to remind everyone that men and women were still fighting overseas and that we mustn't forget them during this season of well-wishes, generosity, and peace. It was a wonderful tribute to a brother and son who would never again attend a Manion Family Christmas Party.

Four months later, he returned home in a flag-draped coffin.

The Manion Family Christmas Party of 2006, when we were blissfully ignorant of the painful loss we would soon come to know, was—to my mom's credit—one of the best. That patriotic tree, which reemerges every Christmas now, exemplifies my mother's spirit. She could stare down fear and worry, almost daring them to make a move.

Janet Manion was tough, optimistic, and focused. She made every decision with self-assurance, as if to spite any concerns or doubts that she may have been harboring. The anxieties, the worries—they were there, of course. They had to be. She simply would not allow them to triumph over her. She had Herculean willpower. For years after Travis's death, my mother continued to be the picture of stalwart strength. She ached in a way that only a mother who has buried her son can, but she never let it keep her down.

It was especially disorienting for me, then, when I learned a few years later that my mother—this pennant of courage for our family—had only eight months to live.

We got the news in 2011, four years after Travis's death. We were already burdened with heavy hearts, but we were together. And frankly, up to that point, we had been managing okay. My parents were spending time in Avalon with me, my husband, and our children. One day, my mom mildly injured her wrist while playing with my little girls on the boardwalk. I took her to the doctor for what we both expected would be a fairly innocuous visit.

No such luck. The scan of her wrist led to more scans and a surgery, which revealed that Stage 4 lung cancer had spread throughout her body.

Eight months later, a few days before the fifth anniversary of Travis's death, my mother joined him in heaven. In only five years, my only sibling and my mother had died. My family of four had been reduced to two.

I was devastated. No marathon was going to make this loss any easier to bear. I had no idea where to turn for help, and I simply couldn't stomach the thought of picking up the pieces once again. I hadn't even collected them all the first time.

In the months after my mother's death on April 24, 2012, I turned to the methods of coping that had become familiar to me: I threw myself into my work and into my family's busy schedule. I set small goals—losing weight, reading, running—anything to keep waking up every day and moving. It had worked before, hadn't it? It could work again, I figured.

I was wrong.

There have been times, in the deepest and most tumultuous moments of grief, when my need for constant activity and focus hasn't served me. In fact, there have been times when being strong, pushing myself to the next milestone, and channeling Travis's discipline and focus have hurt me.

Grief is a savage and shrewd beast that isn't easily tamed. As soon as I found a method of fending off my grief that worked for me, it caught on and found a new mode of attack. Staying goal-oriented and tough-minded got me only so far. Then, the year my mother died, on Christmas night of 2012, it came to find me in my home.

As the holidays approached, that mysterious combination of excitement and dread once again bubbled up inside me. At this point, I had two little girls in school and I manufactured the most convincing smile I could when they brought home holiday-themed art projects. All I could think about was their uncle Travis and grand-mom Janet, who wouldn't get to watch them grow. It was the same bittersweet feeling I'd had the Christmas that Travis deployed for the last time, but this time it was back with a vengeance. I couldn't believe that it would be the first Manion Family Christmas Party we hosted without my mom at the helm. My husband, Dave, who sensed my morose sentimentality and worried where it might lead, gently suggested we take the year off.

"What? No. Of course we're having the Christmas party this year," I responded. This time it was my turn to feel frustrated. And just as my mom had done six years prior, I got to work.

As late December approached, I felt like my old self again. Or at least I convinced myself that I did. After all, my behaviors and expressions were right where I wanted them to be. I was crafting shopping lists, connecting with friends and family, making cookies with the girls, hanging lights, and prepping the house. A few months earlier, I had read somewhere that we should always aim to "Be like a duck": "Remain calm on the surface, but paddle like hell underneath."

Though I wasn't fully aware of it, that was my mental state at the time. My thoughts were almost always racing furiously: a clutter of to-do lists and daily accomplishments that would ultimately reach a fever pitch in the grand masterpiece that would be that year's

Christmas party. And I was fine with that. It was like being twenty-six miles into a run again, positioned at the base of Iwo Jima Hill and prepared to enjoy the second wind that would carry my legs up. I wanted to feel that high again.

And like clockwork, just as I hoped, the feeling came.

On some level, I knew I was still grieving the losses of my brother and mom, but on a much more conscious level, I believed that I had it all figured out. The party was a wild success. I couldn't have been prouder. After everyone had left, I threw the last beer bottle away; when it hit the inside of the can, it sounded like victory.

I can't believe I pulled it off, I thought sleepily. *Mom would be proud.*

All I could think of was the warm, soft bed upstairs. My body was like lead. And when I heaved it onto that glorious mattress, I smiled proudly to myself that I had kept my mother's legacy alive. I closed my eyes and calmly waited for sleep to envelop me.

But sleep didn't come.

Something much nastier arrived in its place. I felt like I received a direct punch to the gut and my eyes immediately sprang open. I started hyperventilating. I couldn't breathe. Pressure was quickly building inside my chest and my mind was on fire with anxiety. It was the most terrifying panic attack I had ever experienced.

"Dave, you have to get me to the hospital," I managed to get out. "I think I'm dying."

I will be forever grateful for what my husband said next.

"No, you're not. Stop, Ryan. Just relax and go to bed."

You might think I'm kidding, but I'm serious. My husband always knows what to say to me when my emotions reach a fever pitch. If I had sensed even the slightest bit of concern in his voice, I know the situation would only have escalated. At the time, however, as you may imagine, I did *not* appreciate it.

I immediately set off into a flurry of accusations that, thankfully, I can no longer remember. Probably something about him not loving me, something about him not understanding—and I'm not proud to admit this, but there may have been some *I hate you*s sprinkled in for good measure.

Dave, the peaceful warrior that he is, remained unfazed and steady. He continued to speak rationally and firmly. It was probably only a few minutes, but they felt like my last. When the intense feelings of anxiety disappeared, and my breathing slowed into a natural rhythm, I had an internal Come-to-Jesus with myself. Clearly, I was not okay.

It was a difficult admission, but I'd managed to stave it off for five years now. It was about time I face the music. Sleep didn't come easily that night. I was shocked that I had reacted this way after what had seemed like such a perfect evening. I had dealt with some minor anxiety before, initially when Travis was deployed and then immediately after his death, but nothing like this. This was positively debilitating.

For the next several months, I was a ghost of my former self. The identity I had painstakingly built for myself after Travis died had shattered. On December 24, 2012, I identified as a tough, capable, resilient woman. I was a marathon runner. I was a dedicated mom and a support-ive wife. I had taken over as executive director of the Travis Manion Foundation, the organization my mother had formed to honor my brother. I led a talented team, and people looked to me for guidance and leadership. And I gave it to them. But December 25 was a different ball game. I was gasping for air and cursing out my exceedingly calm husband.

For months afterward, I was terrified to drive and wouldn't go more than ten miles from my house. I woke up every morning hoping and praying that this would be the day the anxiety would go away. I would force myself to drive to work, but would sit outside my office in my car, hands gripped firmly on the steering wheel, because I couldn't work up the courage to walk in. I was smoking again, and crying in the shower, and regularly feeling seized by anxiety that I simply couldn't shake off. *If this is what life is going to be like from now on*, I thought to myself one day, *I'm done. I can't live like this.*

I knew that I had to do something to help myself or my situation was not going to change, so I started to see a therapist to work through the mental agonies that I had not worked through before. No one but my husband and my best friends Amy and Krista knew what was going on. The calming presence that Dave provided was always a blessing. But something about commiserating with Amy was deeply helpful in putting me back on the path to recovery. Two years earlier, she had lost her husband, Brendan. If there was anyone with whom I felt I could be completely vulnerable, it was her.

I called her one day, overwhelmed and furious. "My therapist diagnosed me with post-traumatic stress disorder today," I shouted into the receiver. "Can you believe that shit? I don't have PTSD!"

To someone who hasn't shared my upbringing, this kind of reaction may sound nonsensical, bordering on insensitive. In my world at that time, ailments were of the body only, not of the mind. And on the off chance that they *were* of the mind, they could be healed by the body.

"Go for a run, Ryan," was my dad's recommendation for solving most of my problems. We didn't put nearly the stock into mental well-being that we did into physical well-being. I am often told that I have a bit of an "icy" demeanor. Showing emotion is not something that comes naturally to me. In fact, crying in front of people makes me feel wildly uncomfortable. Amy, on the other hand, is one of the toughest women I know, but her sweet, mild-mannered nature makes her appear unassuming to most.

She has a beautiful way of showing her vulnerability and has no problem crying in front of others. Maybe it is because, when she cries, she looks like a princess—with delicate tears running down her cheeks. I, on the other hand, am what some would affectionately call an ugly crier. It felt good to sound off to Amy. She always knew what to say when my emotions were ramping up.

"Oh, that's okay, Ryan," she told me. "My therapist told me the same thing."

At that point, we both chuckled, and it dawned on me that there was likely some truth to the diagnosis. Naming my problem didn't do much for me. But sharing it with someone else sure did.

During the following six months, I started to regain my confidence, humor, and peace. I was slowly reclaiming myself. Life slowed down; I focused on my mental health. That did not mean I threw physical challenges out the window. Quite the opposite. I began to understand what my dad meant when he told me to "go for a run" when I wasn't feeling myself. Exercise has a tremendous positive effect on the mind.

This time around, though, I paid attention to the moments when I was feeling anxious or unlike myself. I wasn't pushing toward some far-off, crazy physical goal. Rather, I was using simple exercise as a tool to help with my mental state. The previous five years had been marked by endless, furious motion: always moving to a new target, striving toward a new ambition, crushing my body and exhausting my mind to reach some meaningful goal. I don't regret that approach to grief in the slightest. It was what I needed. It was the method of dealing that was most aligned to my personality, and in many ways it served me.

Until it didn't.

And when I finally allowed myself to slow down and face the beast that had risen up in front of me after the Christmas party of 2012, I gained a perspective I would never trade. I had found the courage to be transformed by my grief. I knew it was going to be a long road from there, but for the first time in years, I wasn't allowing myself to be deceived. It was a tremendous turning point.

It didn't stop me from pushing myself toward tough goals or making impulsive commitments, of course. Such acts are still very much a part of my life. Thankfully, I've since found humor in that tendency. In fact, my characteristic "fearless ignorance" made an appearance on the tenth anniversary of Travis's death. And once again, it was accompanied by a lesson I seem to have to relearn constantly.

One of those lessons occurred on April 29, 2017—a decade after my brother was killed. I had made plans with a group of friends and family, including Amy Looney, to travel to Arlington National Cemetery. I wanted to spend time with my brother in Section 60, where he and Brendan Looney lay side by side.

We were all ready to toast their eternal friendship and selfless sacrifice, and we were all looking forward to sharing fond memories and inside jokes. After the celebration at Arlington we would head to McGarvey's Saloon and Oyster Bar, in Annapolis. It had been a favorite watering hole of Travis and Brendan during their time at the US Naval Academy.

But before any of that, I was going to have to tackle the Manion WOD.

WOD stands for "Workout of the Day," an acronym made famous by the CrossFit community, whose members, for reasons that I only partially understand, take great joy in punishing their bodies with countless repetitions of high-intensity circuit exercises that would leave any mere mortal sore and exhausted.

It's a conditioning program favored by US military service members and *the* favorite of Jimi Letchford, one of Travis's best friends and a fellow Marine who graduated from the Naval Academy. Jimi, who is now director of CrossFit International, had traveled with his wife all the way from the West Coast to join us in marking the anniversary of Travis's death and celebrating his life. Jimi had arranged to do the Manion WOD with a group of midshipmen* at the academy to honor the fallen '04 graduate.

---

* *Midshipmen* is the name given to students at the US Naval Academy in Annapolis.

"Come do it with us!" he texted me the day before. "We've got a spot on the yard,* a great group of mids, and it's gonna be awesome. Come."

I showed the text to Carlo Pecori, with whom Travis had served in the Marine Corps and with whom I had bonded like a brother over the years.

Carlo and I had already arrived in town for the celebration and were pulling together some last-minute logistics for the weekend. We were staying with my dad, who had a home in Annapolis, across the street from the academy.

"I'm in. Will you do it with us?" I asked Carlo.

His furrowed brow and quizzical look produced an expression somewhere between disgust and skepticism. He wasn't exactly jumping at the opportunity.

"Those Hero WODs are no joke, Ryan. You know that, right?"

He probably didn't know this at the time, but there's no better way to get me to do something than to express doubt about my ability to do it. I may have been "in" before. Now I was doubling down. My text back to Jimi read: "I'm in. So is Carlo."

The most grueling CrossFit workouts, I have come to learn, are reserved for Hero WODs. These workouts are dedicated to, and named for, fallen members

---

* "The Yard" is what Annapolis midshipmen call their campus.

of the US military who practiced CrossFit themselves. The numbers and repetitions associated with the workout have significance, and are usually aligned with the hero's date of death. After Travis died, Jimi created the Manion WOD, which consisted of a timed circuit of a four-hundred-meter run and twenty-nine weighted back squats, repeated for seven rounds. It was intended to commemorate Travis's death on 4/29/07. Jimi, who had wrestled on the team with Travis at the academy, designed this workout to be extra brutal on the lower body, since Travis's legs were as strong and solid as tree trunks.

The following morning, I threw on my workout clothes and trotted across the street to The Yard, where I met up with Jimi, his wife Madeline, Carlo, and about fifteen midshipmen. We were ready to face this behemoth of a workout; I was warned that my legs might feel the burn.

Jimi kicked things off with some basic instructions and a review of proper form, as well as some touching words about my brother, the friend that he was, and the ways in which that school had shaped him into the man he became.

I was so proud to stand on the grounds that my brother had once navigated as a student; to stand with his friends who had served, celebrated, and fought with him; and to run alongside the next generation of warriors who would take inspiration from his story of courage and sacrifice. It was an incredible honor. As things got started, I turned to Madeline.

"I have never done squats with weights," I admitted.

"No problem," she assured me. "Just use the bar."

She handed me a long metal bar, the ends of which would normally hold heavy, round weights but which today, thankfully, did not.

"You're using the bar?" This, from Carlo. Incredulous yet again.

"It's not weights, Carlo. It's just a bar." I rolled my eyes.

"You're on your own there. I'm doing air squats. I'm not trying to kill myself." And we were off.

I didn't hold back that day. It had been ten years to the day since I had lost my best friend and I was full of emotions that needed to be channeled somewhere. I wanted to make him proud. I remembered the bench press in the basement, the wooden beam with a list of goals on it, the marathon nearly ten years earlier. And I pushed myself as only Travis could get me to.

Some two hundred back squats and twenty-eight hundred meters of sprints later, I felt amazing. I had given the Manion WOD all I had; there was nothing left in the tank.

"Did you go with the bar the whole time?" Jimi asked me afterward.

"Yeah," I said sheepishly. "I just couldn't do the weights."

"That's badass, Ryan. That thing weighs like forty-five pounds on its own." I shook my head in disbelief. But I was beaming.

As we prepared to leave, I found Carlo throwing up in a trash can outside. I guess he had pushed himself pretty hard, too. We headed back across the street to my parents' house, and all of a sudden it hit me. My quads were seizing up and my legs felt like Jell-O. I was trying to figure out how to walk up the front steps without bending my knees. I waddled like a penguin up each stair, but I made it.

"Carlo, we gotta get to a drugstore. I need some Motrin," I finally told him.

Once we returned to the house, Carlo and I collapsed on adjacent couches, just as Travis and I had done years before in the basement of our Philadelphia home.

Neither of us could move. I'm not sure how long we stayed like that, but it was long enough to watch the movie *Manchester by the Sea*, which is more than two hours long. By the time it ended, I knew we had to start getting ready if we were going to make it to Arlington on time. I finally broke down and texted Jimi.

"Something's wrong," I messaged him. "I don't think I'm supposed to feel like this."

He called me right away. "Where are you?" he asked. "What are you doing?"

I bleakly described what Carlo and I were experiencing.

"You got to move, Ryan!" he said. "You can't lie around. Lactic acid is building up and making it worse. Get off the couch."

I didn't like what I heard, but it didn't matter. He was right. I had to get down to Arlington to meet all our family and friends in Section 60 and then figure out a way to make it to McGarvey's. People were flying in from all over the country to pay their respects and spend time with old friends. *What the hell did you get me into, Travis?*

Two thousand more milligrams of Motrin and I'd be all right. The collateral damage was done for sure, but it was minimal. I had once again found myself punching above my weight and paying for it on the other side. As I showered and got ready for Arlington, I reflected on my decade-long journey of grief. The road had been circuitous: dark, steep, and perilous at times, and somber and serene at others. There were times when I felt I had been traveling alone, and others when I had been fortunate to enjoy the company of friends.

Over the course of those ten years, most things in my life had changed, but some had not. I was still fortunate to be surrounded by those people who had loved and respected my brother the most. I continued to set goals and push my limits in ways that I hoped would make him proud. And, once again, for better or for worse, I was staying busy, occupied, and ambitious in my expectations for myself as a way both to honor my brother's death and to manage the pain that came with it. From the marathon of 2007 to the Manion WOD of 2017, this method had been tried and true for me. It came at a price—most often in the form of an embarrassing and uncomfortable waddle that lasted for several days—but that was a small one to pay.

No matter how dark my days became, or how alone I felt, I always held on to the belief that, if I was honoring my brother's legacy in some small way, then the pain would be worth it. That realization made every daunting task in front of me not just possible, but necessary. I *needed* to honor Travis. I still do. It's an intense compulsion I feel down to my bones. It provides me purpose, and just enough fight to get through the challenges before me. It has been one of the most valuable mechanisms for managing tragedy that I can think of.

With the help of mild painkillers and a commiserating friend, I made it to the celebration at Arlington as well as to the after-party at McGarvey's. The day was perfect. It was more of a raucous reunion than a solemn convening. Any bartender or server would have been shocked to learn the reason for our gathering. It was a rowdy time, characterized by frequent outbursts of laughter, loudly told stories, and warm recollections of years past that endeared us to one another. My chest swelled with gratitude and a strong pride for the community my brother had created.

At one point, Amy and I walked outside of the bar.

We wanted a quiet moment away from the crowd to simply be. We wanted to take in the moment and pause to appreciate how far we'd come together. I couldn't help but notice that the weather was almost exactly the same as it had been ten years ago to the day, unseasonably warm and full of sun. Standing there in Annapolis brought back so many memories for both of us. It was the place Amy and I had first met, when Travis introduced her to me as Brendan's new girlfriend.

We caught ourselves in a moment of disbelief that here we were in the city that had shaped so much of who Travis and Brendan were—and they were not here with us. Even our friendship might never have developed had it not been for the two people we loved and lost. The entire day was a testament to Travis's character: The relationships he had forged in life were made only stronger in his death. As I looked back at the dozens of close friends and family at my side, I could almost feel that line graph spiking dramatically upward. I was truly happy.

And this is the secret to getting off the hedonic treadmill. The fact is, it's a natural impulse to find yourself on it again and again, searching for that unmatched high that will bring you joy. If you look down and see your feet moving rapidly and you're going nowhere fast, don't fret. It happens. But if you are intentional about it, you don't need to remain on there forever.

To break away from that unforgiving pattern, you

need to do one very important thing: You have to be honest with yourself. No more self-deception. For a long time, I had lied to myself about how happy and fulfilled I felt. Frankly, it was easier that way. I even lied about the things that made me feel happy and fulfilled: *If I just stay busy*, I would think. Maybe the story you tell yourself is a little different:

"If I just lose a few more pounds"... "If I just earn a few more thousand dollars a year"... "If I can just get that guy to notice me..."

"*Then* I'll be happy. *Then* I'll be okay."

When we shed those deceptive stories we tell ourselves, we create a space where we are able to see what actually does make us authentically happy. I bet you'll find you weren't totally off. As I said, we all seek the same things: love, acceptance, purpose. We just look for them in the wrong places. When I stood with Amy outside McGarvey's, I knew that I had found them: a sense of community, friendship, growth. They were all right there, laid out in front of me. And it was because I took a moment of quiet, away from the activity and the chaos, that I got to experience and appreciate it in an intentional and meaningful way.

Intention was the key that I'd been missing. I was so caught up in goals and milestones and challenges and ambitions that I'd missed the simple but profound element that makes everything worthwhile. And the fact is, I'm still hungry. I'm still ambitious. I'm still a fighter. I still like to push my body to do things I may not quite be ready for, and hell yes, I've still got goals and dreams.

But now, I also have something else. I have intention. The year 2012 was the most painful and difficult of my life. But it taught me some of the most important lessons around intention. I believe that the single greatest key to resilience is setting *intentional goals*. Both words of that phrase are important, and I've learned you can't have one without the other. We'll take *goals* first.

Goals are what remind us that life goes on. We need them to keep us waking up and getting out of bed every morning, even when we'd much rather stay in bed with the door locked, the lights out, and our heads safely under the covers. Goals—no matter how small— are what remind us that life is a process and that we are always growing and becoming better. They keep us hopeful and orient us toward the future. However, they are not enough on their own; they must be made and executed with intention.

Achieving a goal for the sake of vainglory and sheer accomplishment will bring satisfaction—but that satisfaction will prove to be short-lived. Achieving goals that have deep meaning to us will bring us far more happiness. When we set goals that have meaning outside of our own selfish ends, we discover it's not about the destination; it's about the journey.

Whenever I set out to do something that honors the

legacy of Travis, whether it's simple like completing a workout, or more valuable, like serving the needs of another, I treat the activity differently than I would anything else. After all, it's for Travis. I want to give it my full attention and focus. I become absorbed in the process and present in the moment. I act with intention.

Adding intention into my daily living was a powerful shift for me. Goal setting had always come naturally to me. It requires fearlessness and passion, and I'm comfortable with both. But intentionality was another story. That required me to slow down; to be comfortable with silence, peace, and presence. That was far more difficult. Along the road to intention, I came across countless bumps and pitfalls, but I also learned a few valuable truths.

FIRST, DON'T USE A JACKHAMMER
WHEN A CHISEL WILL DO.

When I saw a problem in front of me, I went at with a jackhammer. I was convinced that if I applied enough force to it, I could make it go away. But some problems, even big ones, need only a well-deployed chisel. Intention is the chisel.

I was introduced to intention when my mom received her eight-month prognosis. Travis's young life had been ripped from mine violently and quickly, but in the case of my mom, I was given the opportunity to say my goodbyes. I asked her questions about her life and wrote down her responses. We spent every day together, and she held my girls every chance she got.

After she died and all that disappeared, I believed, for a time, that I had been robbed. I was heartbroken and right back where I had started. But then I relearned a lesson on intentionality. I was crudely reminded of how short, sweet, and precious our lives are.

To this day, I never board a plane or head to a business trip without kissing my children goodbye. I (try) never to go to bed without resolving some conflict with my husband. I never take for granted the precious, limited moments I have with the people I love, and when I'm with them, I make it my intention to let them know how important they are to me.

I've never considered the idea that losing half of my family could have given me a competitive edge, but maybe I ought to. I know the cost of not having the opportunity to say or do what matters most—and I refuse to squander the blessings that I have been given. I choose to live with intention.

SECOND, IT'S NOT "EITHER/OR." IT'S "BOTH/AND."

Let me be clear: Intention is not meant to replace goals and ambitions. It's meant to color them. Committing to vigorous feats—physical, mental, or otherwise—is often good in its own right. Maybe you want to pass those boards, or crush that personal-best time, or compete for that promotion. These are all good things. These aims are fueled by discipline and focus. But they are nourished by intention.

There's no goal worth pursuing that can't be enjoyed. If your goals can be easily achieved and represent nothing more than stepping-stones toward the next goals, then you are in a rat race.

Difficult-to-attain goals and accomplishments are what keep our heart rates up and our blood pumping. They give us life. But intention is what gives our lives meaning. It's what makes life worth living.

FINALLY, FAILURE IS A BRUISE, NOT A TATTOO.

Before Travis died, I never bothered to think much about failure. That's not because I was wildly successful at everything I tried my hand at. Believe me, I failed at plenty of things. Rather, it was because I didn't care enough about anything to give it much effort. I was sometimes apathetic. Travis was the ambitious, goal-oriented one; I was just coasting through life. After he died, and then my mom died, I had a major wake-up call. Now I feel compelled to take advantage of the time I have left on this earth to lead a life they both can be proud of.

I want to do this not for my sake, but for theirs. After their deaths, goals fueled me, intention nourished me, and I became obsessed with finding the next mountain to climb. I would let nothing stop me from getting to the top. But then, as occurs with all humans, I failed. I had no idea how to deal with failure, since I had never permitted myself to deal with it before.

Failure can be crushing. It can make you feel worthless and disillusioned. The first few times I failed, I simply was not prepared for the consequences. I had become so programmed to forge ahead and not let anything stop me that I did not know how to handle it when I hit a roadblock.

For a time, I allowed my failures to define me. Then I began to accept them as simply a stage in the process. Failure wasn't so scary anymore. When we recognize that our lives are just a series of successes and failures, we are more likely to be able to handle difficulties when they arise. And they always do. Eventually, despite the inevitable failures, we come to learn that our next success is never too far off in the distance.

Ryan Manion and her husband, Dave, with their three children, Maggie Rose, Honor Emma, and Travis Brendan.

Ryan's best friend, Krista, with Travis, circa 1999. The girls were forever trying to convince Travis to join them in a bit of trouble.

Ryan with her dad, Colonel Tom Manion, at the start line of the Marine Corps Marathon in 2007.

Travis and Ryan getting ready for a night out in Los Angeles in 2006, right before his second deployment to Iraq.

Ryan with her daughter Maggie Rose in 2007, four months after Travis's death and still wearing that red USMC sweatshirt.

Travis and Ryan circa 1984.

Ryan's son, Travis Brendan, standing between the graves of his uncle and his uncle's best friend, in Section 60 of Arlington National Cemetery.

One of the last pictures ever taken of Travis, while on
deployment in Iraq, 2007.

Amy and Brendan Looney at a Bruce Springsteen concert in Washington, DC.

Amy and Joel Heffernan, at their wedding ceremony in Chicago, IL.

Amy, Brendan, and Travis Manion, at the wedding of a mutual friend after graduation in 2004, in Texas.

Brendan's last deployment, in Afghanistan, 2010. You can see an adopted puppy peering from the rucksack at his hip.

Travis Brendan Borek and Brendan Travis Looney, serving as ring bearers at the wedding of Amy and Joel.

One of the last photos taken of Rob
Kelly, November 2010, by combat
cameraman LCpl Dexter Saulisbury,
in Sangin, Afghanistan.

Rob and Heather
renewing their
vows—for the third
time—while on their
honeymoon in Las
Vegas, July 3, 2007.

Rob and Heather on their wedding day, June 30, 2007, Quantico, VA.

Rob on his final deployment, to Sangin,
Afghanistan, with 3rd Battalion, 5th Marines.

Heather at the Travis Manion Foundation's 9/11 Heroes Run 5k in San Diego, 2014. a year prior to joining the Foundation as a staff member

Heather and Melissa on an adventure to Las Vegas, February 2012.

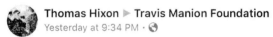

Thomas Hixon ▶ Travis Manion Foundation
Yesterday at 9:34 PM · 🌐

My father, a victim of the Parkland shooting, ran towards building 1200 as soon as the sound of gunshots rang out. He attempted to confront and disarm the shooter and gave his life in the process. When my mother and I sat down to think of what to put on his headstone we both decided there was no better motto to put than Travis'. Semper Fidelis.

A Facebook post sent to the Travis Manion Foundation in March 2018 by Thomas Hixon, to honor his father, killed in the Parkland school shooting the month before.

Nine months later, Thomas Hixon (in the black tux) stands on the bar singing along with his Travis Manion Foundation family.

Ryan, Heather, and Amy in La Jolla, CA, 2019.

Amy

CHAPTER 4

Tuesday, September 21, 2010

I woke up to find an email sitting in my inbox from my husband, Brendan. He must have written it in the middle of the night. The subject line read, "Almost Home!" I was always excited to get word from him, but especially lately. I couldn't believe Brendan was going to be back in only a matter of weeks. I'd been waiting for his return for more than six months while he and his SEAL team were deployed to Afghanistan. I was ready for it to be over, and the email was a nice reminder that it would be soon.

It was also a welcome break from all the work-related emails I'd found myself buried under the past few weeks. I was so overwhelmed. I had started a new job just three months earlier and was working sixty to seventy hours per week, trying to establish my territory selling medical devices for rehabilitating patients.

I was barely awake when I glanced at my inbox that morning, but my mind was alert enough to read his short note hungrily. Our communication was limited, so I always savored whatever messages I received. Along with his regular, sweet sentiments checking in on me and sharing his anticipation about coming back to our little California townhome and two rambunctious dogs, he had a favor to ask. Brendan was nothing if not a loyal and selfless friend, so not surprisingly, the favor was for someone else.

His friend Andrew, with whom he had played lacrosse at the Naval Academy, had just arrived in Afghanistan. Andrew was with SEAL Team Four and was relieving Brendan, on SEAL Team Three. As the assistant officer in charge, or AOIC, Brendan was turning things over to Andrew and wanted to make sure he had everything he needed—including peace of mind—to do his job well.

The email went on to say that Andrew was recently married with a young child. His wife, Marissa, was living at their home in Virginia Beach. Brendan was still trying to track down Marissa's contact info, but he wanted me to reach out and check in on her. Brendan and I had done a couple of deployments together at this point and we knew how rocky and unsettling things can be for a couple the first time through.

"Can you just call her? Or shoot her an email?" he wrote. "Just give her some hope about this deployment. I think it will really put Andrew's mind at ease, too."

I wasn't surprised that, even amid all the chaos of winding down his own deployment and handing the reins over to another team, this was top of mind for Brendan. He believed that family was the most important thing, and you can't do your job well or complete a combat mission successfully if you're worried about what's going on at home thousands of miles away.

Brendan and I had an unspoken rule: We never burdened each other with whatever concerns were weighing on our minds. If I told him about the stresses of my new job, I know he would just spend more time thinking about them and wishing he could help me. I would rather have him focus on finishing this deployment safely and coming home to me.

And he knew better than to tell me about the fifty-eight combat missions he'd been on until that point in his career. That would undoubtedly launch a stream of sleepless nights for me.

"There's no sense worrying about things you can't control," he often reminded me. "And unfortunately, you can't control what happens when I'm deployed. You can hope, you can pray, but there are some things you just can't control."

The funny thing is, my Navy SEAL husband had somehow convinced me that he worked at a desk, even when he was deployed to Afghanistan. It's surprising, when I think back now, how naive I allowed myself to be. But Brendan was just as humble as he was protective, so it was typical of him to downplay his routine.

"What did you do today?" I'd ask him on the rare occasions we were able to talk on the phone during deployment.

"Oh, you know. Worked out, hung with the dudes, chilled. Did some paperwork, knocked out a little work in the office, that sorta thing."

He was always pretty vague in those conversations, and I was happy to accept what he said at face value. Ignorance was bliss. And he was right. If I had known what he was *really* doing, it only would have worried me. I finished reading his email and made a mental note to reach out to Marissa as soon as he got back to me with her contact information. In the meantime, though, I was late for work.

I had scheduled an 8 a.m. appointment with a patient, which was an earlier jump on the day than I was used to. By seven thirty, I was out the door and on my way to the patient's home.

Once there, as I fitted the gentleman, an older patient, for a splint, he launched into a long story about his sister. She had just died, and he felt terribly lonely without her. I felt sorry for the man and I didn't want to be impolite, so I stayed and chatted with him longer than I normally would. I remember thinking to myself, *I'm sorry about your sister, sir. But it's nearly 10 a.m. and I've got other appointments. Can we try and wrap this up?*

It's strange for me to recollect that and realize what little tolerance I had for another person's pain at that point in my life. With the exception of Brendan's best friend, Travis, who was killed in Iraq, I had never known the grief of losing a loved one. If I had known that, at that very moment, uniformed members of the Navy were knocking on the door to my empty townhome, perhaps I would have reacted differently toward my patient.

I was grateful to leave the gentleman, but confused when I looked down at my phone. I had several missed calls from our corporate office and a voicemail from Brendan's Navy command asking me to return the call. I also had several texts from friends on the West Coast. They were all wondering if I'd heard from Brendan.

My heart sank. *This can't be good.* I got in my car and decided to call work back first, since I wasn't prepared to deal with the others. When I reached the main office, I heard the friendly voice of Loretta, our office administrator.

"Hey, Amy. Yeah, so this guy from the Navy kept calling trying to reach you."

I immediately felt like I was going to throw up.

Shaking, I took a deep breath. "Well," I managed to get out. "What did he say?"

"I think everything's fine," Loretta told me. I let out a sigh of relief. *Okay, so whatever it is, it can't be that bad.* "But he'd like to meet with you. I told him about the conference our company is having in La Jolla, about twenty-five minutes from where you are right now, and he said you should meet him there."

I hung up the phone feeling a little better. "Everything is fine," I reminded myself. She seemed calm, right? And after listening to the voicemail from Navy command, I figured the caller sounded pretty composed, too. I clung to these two conclusions because I needed to believe they were true.

I typed the hotel address into my GPS. Loretta was right: It was estimating twenty-five minutes with traffic. As soon as I started to drive, however, my overactive brain kicked into gear and revealed just how uncertain and scared I was. I felt hot and then weak and then nauseated. I couldn't calm myself and took every wrong turn available to me. I was very confused, and my mind was racing. I couldn't focus on anything for more than a few seconds. I tried calling my sister-in-law, Ali, who lived nearby, but she didn't pick up. I left a distracted voicemail asking her to go immediately to the hotel in La Jolla to meet me. The twenty-five-minute drive took me an hour and a half. The only way I got through it was by convincing myself that Brendan was injured and

I'd be flying to Germany later that day to meet him at the hospital and nurse him back to health.

I knew I couldn't even fathom, much less handle, Brendan being gone.

Finally, I turned down the street to the hotel. Once it was in sight, I abandoned my car—leaving the door open, keys in the ignition, purse in plain sight—in the middle of the street. At this point, I wasn't thinking; I was merely reacting. I rushed into the lobby, which was full of men in full dress military uniforms. As soon as they spotted me, their conversations stopped dead. Their expressions were pained. That's when I knew the truth. Brendan wasn't coming back.

Before they could say anything, I burst into tears. Ali had made it to the hotel before I had, and when I spotted her in the lobby, she started sobbing. Everyone, including co-workers, had been waiting for me because I'd told them I would only be twenty-five minutes. I'm sure they had started to worry, since it took me well over an hour.

I couldn't tell you what happened in that hour if I tried. I don't remember it at all. I could have easily killed someone on the road, and to this day that thought makes me sick. My cries echoing throughout the lobby were so loud and uncontrolled that I'm sure I was making a terrible scene. But I didn't care.

Members of Brendan's Navy command, as well as Ali and a few co-workers, escorted me into a hotel guest room to ensure our conversation would be private. I think I threw up either in the hotel room or on the way to it, but even that is a blur to me now. As soon as we crammed into the room, I sat on the corner of a plush, king-size bed. The room felt hollow and sterile. I looked at the boring art hanging on the neutral-colored walls and felt far away from what was happening around me.

It was there, hunched at the foot of the bed, that I received official notification from two uniformed service members that my husband, Navy Lieutenant Brendan Looney, had been killed in Afghanistan. He and eight others had died in a helicopter crash the night before—not long after he had sent the email. My co-workers and my sister-in-law held me as I seized with overpowering sobs.

What no one tells you about losing a loved one unexpectedly is that emotions—as raw and intense as they may be at that time—quickly take a backseat to planning and logistics. Thankfully, Ali, who was married to Brendan's brother, was an absolute warrior during the whole process. She saw to it that I was driven home from the hotel. On the way to our town house, she called every friend Brendan or I had and instructed them, "Drop what you're doing. Go to Amy and Brendan's place right now. We need people there and we're going to need help with everything."

When I arrived back at the town house, it no longer

felt like home, even though it was filled with the love of our West Coast military family. The people there—through no fault of their own—couldn't fill the void left behind by the one I'd lost. They wanted to be close to me, even if it was just to sit on the couch and stare blankly ahead at another episode of *How I Met Your Mother.*

No one seemed to know what to do or say. We gathered in my living room, where I'm sure there was plenty of conversation, but I don't know that I joined in any of it. I was too busy checking my phone every five minutes, certain that I'd receive a text from Brendan. I truly believed that at any moment he'd send me a note apologizing for the confusion and assuring me that everything was okay. I didn't care what the uniformed men had said. There was no way that Brendan really was gone forever.

Still, I was grateful that the home was not empty, and that there were plenty of capable people around to make decisions for me. At that point, I was incapable of making them myself. During the course of the day, Ali spent hours handling phone calls and navigating difficult conversations since I had no interest in talking to anyone outside immediate family.

I felt bad that I couldn't talk to everyone who was calling to express their condolences, but I simply wasn't in the frame of mind to console others. I could barely handle my own thoughts. For the next few hours, Ali and I scrambled to reschedule the work meetings and appointments I had coming up. I couldn't think straight and I needed help accomplishing even the smallest tasks. I was pacing around my bedroom trying to figure out what I was supposed to do next. Was I supposed to go somewhere? How would I get there? What would I pack? Was I expected to tell other people now? How did this work?

The Navy had assigned me a casualty assistance officer to help answer these questions. He had been there in the hotel with us and had gone to our townhome, too, but I hadn't even noticed him at first. Ali spoke with him in hushed tones out in the hallway and then came to find me pacing in my bedroom.

"We have to fill out some paperwork, Amy," she said. Then she led me down the hall like I was a small child. I was grateful to have someone parent me in that moment.

Together we worked through the paperwork that had to be completed immediately, and she somehow managed to furnish the officers with important documents—wills and power-of-attorney statements—that she found upstairs in a labeled folder. She knew where all my clothes were and went through my closet to pack a bag for me.

The Navy had booked me on a red-eye flight to the East Coast that would depart that night. Everything was happening so quickly. I was to arrive at 7 a.m. the next day in Philadelphia, where I would meet my mom and sister at the airport.

From there, we would drive seventy-two miles to Dover Air Force Base, Delaware, where I would join Brendan's family and Travis's family to greet my husband's body when it arrived from Afghanistan.

Just a few hours earlier, as I scanned Brendan's email, I had been excitedly anticipating a joyous reunion with my husband. And now I was dreading a torturous, and final, goodbye.

I'm not even thirty years old and I'm a widow.

That's all I could think about as I stared out the window on the five-hour flight from San Diego to Philadelphia. Even the word *widow* made me shudder. It evoked an image of a gray-haired, hunched-over woman dressed in black. *One day*, I thought, *my blond hair will turn silver and my straight spine will shrivel up. Then I'll look the part. Until then*, I figured, *I'll just spend the next few decades biding my time, waiting for that day to come.* Things were looking overwhelmingly bleak.

I had never planned on marrying young. Brendan knew that. I was the product of divorced parents and had been raised by a single mother who worked eighty hours each week to support me and my sister. I respected my mom's work ethic, but I was scared of making an ill-informed decision in my twenties that I'd have to live with for the rest of my life.

And then, of course, I met Brendan. "Twenty-five is

too young to marry," I told him when we first talked about marriage. I hadn't considered that I'd be alone again at twenty-nine.

The entire experience was surreal. Instead of preparing to kiss my husband for the first time in nearly seven months, I was on my way east to meet a body. On the airplane, when that thought hit me, my brain froze. I was confused. I couldn't process what was happening. How do you prepare to make decisions after losing your spouse so young? How do you say goodbye to the one person around whom you had planned your entire future?

Those first few weeks, I felt like a child, passively accepting plans that others were making for me. I worried that I wasn't in the right mind-set to make rational decisions about what to do next. As someone who prides herself on being decisive and independent, I found myself in an incredibly difficult place. I had lots of other people to think of, including Brendan's relatives, and I wanted to do right by him. I wanted to make decisions—about his funeral, about his burial— that I would feel good about decades down the road.

And yet I was also convinced this was all happening to someone else. I spent much of that plane ride still wondering if the news about Brendan's death was just a huge mistake that someone would correct when we touched down in Philly.

Reality didn't hit me, in fact, until I saw Brendan's

body. To see my husband lying lifeless was the hardest thing I'd ever experienced. I looked down at him in the casket, and I knew it was my Brendan. But he looked distorted. His skin was sallow and his bone structure misaligned. I later learned that his neck had been broken in the helicopter crash that killed him. Of the nine men on that helicopter, only one had survived. It was Andrew, the teammate whom Brendan had emailed me about the day before, asking me to check on his wife.

At Dover, I greeted Brendan's parents and siblings and our friends and family who had gathered to welcome him home. Janet Manion had lost her son, Travis, Brendan's best friend, only three years before. She held me tightly. I could feel her heart breaking all over again when she looked at me. We hugged, and as we endured a stretch of intense, shared pain, I had the first clear thought I'd had in twenty-four hours. It was the only decision I remember making in the early days after Brendan died, but it was the best one I could have made.

Suddenly, a lightbulb went off: Travis and Brendan would be buried together, I decided. That was what needed to happen. I told Janet what I wanted, and she looked confused and sympathetic, as though I were a lost child whom she wasn't quite sure how to help.

"But Amy, honey, Travis is buried in Pennsylvania at our family plot."

"Fine," I remember saying. "Then Brendan will be with him."

Janet's expression immediately shifted. Her characteristic self-assurance shone in her eyes. And she wasn't looking at me with sympathy anymore. She was looking at me with respect.

"Okay, then," she said. "That's what we'll do. But it won't be in Pennsylvania. That wouldn't be right." I was taken aback by this last part. "We'll move Travis to Arlington and bury him there. Brendan will be right by his side."

I didn't realize it at the time, but there were a number of hurdles we'd have to jump in order to make all this happen. Moving Travis's remains required approvals from the secretary of the army, who oversaw Arlington National Cemetery, as well as from the secretary of defense. And it would mean that Travis's re-interment would need to take place within days so that Brendan could be buried beside him immediately after. I didn't lift a finger to make any of this happen, but within forty-eight hours, it was settled. Travis would be moved to Arlington on a Friday, and Brendan would be laid to rest beside him the following Monday.

The drive from Dover to Brendan's parents' home in Maryland was a long and somber one. It was the heavy calm before the storm that was about to erupt. My head hurt from hours of crying and lack of sleep, but I was ready for the hustle and bustle that I knew would greet me at the Looney home. Brendan was one of six children, and he had many close cousins, teammates,

SEAL buddies, neighbors, and friends who wanted to be close to us during this time.

Bring on the chaos, I thought to myself as we pulled into the Looneys' driveway. *Anything will be better than the heavy solitude of the last twenty-four hours.*

The friendly, rambunctious environment of the Looney home did not disappoint. Those first few days were a true Irish wake. There seemed to be hundreds of people filing in and out of the house at all hours of the night and day, a never-ending revolving door of chatty mourners.

I appreciated the activity around me, but I also felt separate from it. As I looked from room to room, I felt as though I were looking through a glass wall. I turned toward the kitchen. People were belly laughing as one of Brendan's SEAL buddies told a wildly inappropriate story about a drunken night in Thailand.

I glanced over at the living room. A lacrosse teammate was proposing a toast to Brendan and people were alternating between wiping away tears, chuckling at old memories, and clinking together aluminum beer cans.

Many of my girlfriends from middle school, high school, and college came by, too. We'd sit together on the porch, sometimes talking, sometimes not. I hadn't seen some of them since my wedding day.

What a different scene this was. We all felt powerless and confused, and no one seemed to know how to act. There's no rulebook for how to interact with your twenty-something girlfriend after her husband dies, so we all just did the best we could and tried to at least enjoy the fact that we were all gathered together.

I was so grateful when I saw Ryan Manion walk through the door of the Looney home. Here was someone who had some understanding of the pain I felt. It had been three years since she lost her brother, Travis, and I'm sure that the loss of his best friend opened up old wounds for her.

I gave her a long hug. Ali approached to break up our embrace because she was ready to get down to business. Ali was like a watchdog on the lookout for anything that would ease my grief. She was ten steps ahead of me, anticipating problems I didn't even know were on the horizon, and solving them before they reached me.

"Ryan," Ali cut in as she gave her a quick embrace. "Those big, dark sunglasses you wore to Travis's funeral? Where did you get them? Amy needs a pair."

Another woman might have been caught off guard by a question like that. She had just walked in the door to comfort a grieving friend and was immediately interrogated about an outfit she had worn three years prior. But like most people who have lived through the pain of tragedy, Ryan knew better. She understood that there were practical concerns in play that needed to be addressed just as much as emotional ones.

"Oh yeah, those were great," Ryan responded. "You're definitely going to want a pair like those. I was bawling my eyes out all during Travis's funeral. No one wants to be seen in that state. I can help find something."

These are the things you simply don't think about when you're making arrangements for your twenty-nine-year-old husband's funeral and burial. It was a gift to have people surrounding me who could consider the little details that my overwhelmed brain could not.

I trusted Ali with any wardrobe decisions from there and rejoined the activity of the Looney household. Beers were poured, Saint Brendan's Irish Cream Liqueur was passed, and stories of Brendan's heroism and humor echoed in every corner of the house. Finally, in the late hours of the night or the early hours of the next morning, everyone found a couch or bed to sleep on. We would drift to sleep feeling warm and nostalgic, only to wake up feeling heavy and burdened. It went on like this for days as we ran down the clock toward Brendan's funeral and burial service.

I stayed at the Looney home all week, but I didn't sleep much. Whatever sleep I did get was of poor quality. I've never been much of a drinker, but I don't think I spent a sober night in that house in the days after Brendan died. I wasn't even eating at that point, but you could always find me with a drink in my hand. Of course, I'd heard of people trying to drown their sorrows with alcohol, but I don't think I believed that's what I was doing at the time. I never would have articulated it that way anyway. I, along with everyone else, was simply caught up in the celebration of Brendan's life. It felt good and familiar to be around people who knew and loved my husband. They wanted to share their piece of Brendan's life with me—how he had affected them, how he had pushed them to be better, how he had made them laugh—and I soaked it up like a sponge.

I didn't want those toasts or those stories to end, because every time I heard his name I felt that Brendan was still with me. He was still alive for those of us in that house. Every beer that clinked and foamed over was affirmation that my husband was real; that he shared a past not just with me, but with each person in the room; that he was loved and respected; and that the world really was a worse place without him in it. The cloudy haze of nonstop drinking and constant company I found myself in that week was all that made the nightmare I'd been living bearable.

When Friday arrived, it was time to inter Travis at Arlington. The Manion family had wanted a quiet ceremony as they moved his remains from Pennsylvania, where he'd been laid to rest three years earlier. Ryan, Travis's sister, tried to make me swear that I wouldn't go to the ceremony. She wanted to make sure I took that time to prepare for my husband's burial three days later.

But of course, there was no way I was going to miss it. It was a chilly fall day, and as I stood outside with a shawl wrapped around my shoulders, I stared in disbelief as they lowered the casket of my husband's best friend into the ground. I felt completely empty. In three days, Brendan would be joining him there forever.

Much to the surprise of the Manion family, the ceremony was anything but quiet. The family arrived to find about 250 Marines from Marine Corps Base Quantico in full dress uniform standing reverently at the burial site. Dozens of Travis's and Brendan's closest friends and family members showed up to pay their respects. Nothing those two did in life had ever been restrained or mild, so why should their funerals be any different?

Eventually, we all ended up at McGarvey's Bar in Annapolis, a favorite spot of Travis and Brendan, and later Brendan and me. We spent many a night together at McGarvey's.

Being back on our old stomping grounds so soon after Brendan died had a strange effect on me. We walked in the door and immediately I was done. I was done putting on a pleasant face and playing the role of polite hostess. I was done navigating the emotions of others at the expense of my own. I was done having people look at me with big, watery eyes like I was a fragile puppy in need of care. I grabbed Ryan, my sister-in law Ali, my friend Lindsey, and a couple other girlfriends and headed for a secluded space in the bar behind the stairs. I needed a break from the crowd.

Within minutes, after ordering a round of shots, we were all holding up our glasses and looking at each other with halfhearted smiles and shrugs. *In a few hours, I bury my husband and my life resets to zero*, I thought to myself. *Here goes nothing.*

I swallowed the liquor and felt my shoulders relax. A few minutes later, another round appeared. And then another one. The next thing I knew, we were back to planning what I would be wearing to my husband's funeral. *How the hell is this happening right now?* was all I could think. Ali, who had played every role from chauffeur to executive assistant to legal counsel over the past week, was now acting in the role of stylist.

"Oh, Ryan, I found those sunglasses," she said. "I got the biggest, darkest, buggiest ones I could find. I think we're good there."

"Thank God," I said. The liquor had made my tone a little more abrasive than I'd intended. "I might be crying my eyes out, but the last thing I need is people looking at me like I'm some naive, pathetic little girl. If people start fawning all over me with pity, it's just going to piss me off. I know what I signed up for and so did Brendan. I just don't want people to feel sorry for me, you know?"

I sighed and took another gulp of my drink. I couldn't believe this was where life had taken me.

Brendan's funeral at Arlington the following Monday morning was beautiful, moving, and painful. It was pouring rain and we had a tent assembled that could only hold two or three rows of chairs near the casket for family. I sat in the front and barely took my eyes off the wooden box holding my husband. When the ceremony concluded, a line of fellow SEALs with whom Brendan had served formed by the casket. They removed from their uniforms the trident lapel pins that they'd received upon graduation from SEAL training.

Then one by one, each SEAL stepped up to the casket and pounded his pin into the wooden frame, where it would remain buried forever with Brendan. The loud, hammering sound became rhythmic, like a drumbeat. And each time I heard the metal pin being driven into the casket, I shook a little and lost my breath for a moment. Each hammered pin felt like a stab in my heart.

When the last trident had been pounded in, I took one last look. I still couldn't believe that it was my Brendan who was inside that casket. When it was time to leave him behind, I felt an intense pang of guilt. I glanced over at Travis's grave site beside my husband.

Typical Travis, I thought. *Setting the bar exceedingly high.*

And typical Brendan. I looked back at my husband's final resting place. *Always rising to meet it.*

I gave one long, last look. Everything felt so heavy and final. I closed my eyes and took a deep breath. I could take solace in knowing that they'd always be together. In this whole mess, I knew I'd done at least one thing right.

Pretty soon after, it was time to return to our home in

California. Our dogs had been in the care of my friend Lindsey for nearly three weeks now, and it wouldn't be right to ask her to keep them much longer. I was going to have to find a way to keep living, and if only for my dogs' sakes, I might as well start sooner rather than later.

But when I returned to our empty townhome, where Brendan's clothes still hung in the closet and our wedding photo was displayed on the mantel, I realized just how difficult the task to keep living would be.

Anyone who knows me knows that I'm usually a highly motivated, highly disciplined, Type A personality. My closet is color-coded. My appointment book is expertly maintained. I send a thank-you card no more than seventy-two hours after receiving a favor. But the loss of a loved one throws you into a tailspin that doesn't simply redefine your routine. It shatters it.

Back in San Diego, anything I had once thought I cared about couldn't have been further from my mind. I lay on my couch in pajamas watching the 2 p.m., 4 p.m., *and* 6 p.m. showings of whatever movie was playing on Lifetime. I was constantly throwing away full trays of food that had been delivered by concerned friends and neighbors. I wasn't hungry—and besides, with whom was I going to eat an entire tray of lasagna? It was just another sad reminder that I was utterly alone. I went days without brushing my teeth. I stayed up to weird hours of the night and then swallowed pills to fall asleep.

Even our beloved dogs couldn't bring me back to life.

The poor things got no exercise or sunshine in those early weeks. I sat and watched apathetically as, day after day, they peed in a corner of the living room and trotted away.

I had no schedule and was accountable to no one. It was no way to live. Not until I forced myself to create a schedule did I begin to feel a shred of my old self again. Sometimes the schedule simply said, "Meet a friend for lunch today." And it took every ounce of my strength and discipline to actually do it. But when I did—when I showered and put on real clothes and forced myself outside and into a conversation with a friend—I felt human again.

It was four months before I went back to work. For a long time, I couldn't bring myself to drive anywhere, which was non-negotiable for a career like mine in medical sales.

It was a few more months before I could force myself to exercise or meet up with friends after work. It was much easier to stick to my diet of Ambien, pajamas, and a dark room as soon as I got home.

After a long day at work, all I wanted to do was go home and be myself. Unfortunately, as soon as I got there, the loneliness set in and I became acutely aware of how eerily quiet everything was. The silence was deafening. I had barely any willpower, but I'd preserved just enough self-respect to know that what I was doing to myself wasn't good.

It occurred to me that I probably should take out my dogs so they wouldn't pee in the house, and that I was forming an unhealthy attachment to sleeping pills. I didn't like the zombie I'd become. Most of all, I knew Brendan would have hated to see me in this state. More than saddening him, it would have disappointed him. I couldn't stomach the thought of that. He had always pushed me and challenged me to operate outside my comfort zone. He constantly reminded me how strong and tough I was. And even though I didn't feel strong or tough, I supposed I could fake it, for his sake.

The events of September 21, 2010, and the subsequent weeks are not a coherent or linear memory to me. There are days and days that I cannot account for. I'm able to share them now only because I've spent years piecing together accounts from various friends and a few blurry recollections of my own. For many years, not remembering was the only way I could live.

I found plenty of help: Ambien at bedtime, shots at McGarvey's, and beers at the Looney house. I was grateful for any agent that would lighten my load or cloud my memory.

In the years that followed, I found a new way to cope: I became expert in the skill of compartmentalization. It was as though the death of my loving husband was not my story at all. It was the fate of some very unfortunate girl, and I could watch her from a distance, completely unaffected. Eventually, I returned to color-coding my closet, shooting out thank-you cards at lightning speed, and diligently maintaining my appointment book. The casual observer never would have known the trauma I'd experienced, and I much preferred it that way. The painful memories were locked tightly away in a vault that I had no plans ever to reopen.

Writing this book, however, has empowered me to reopen that vault. I'm still sifting through all the contents inside, and by no means have I sorted them all out. But every day, I unpack a little more and I become more whole as a result. I'm proud of where I am now, but I also know that every day is different. Tomorrow I may hear our song "Clocks" on the radio and choke back tears on my commute to work.

In a month, I may remember that it's the anniversary of the day we bought our home in California and turn into a puddle again. Each day is different, so I take them all one at a time. But if there's anything my late husband taught me, it's to never give up.

"Be strong. Be accountable. Never complain." That was Brendan's catchphrase of sorts. He had it written on a whiteboard above his desk and he'd repeat it to himself often. Those words are simple, straightforward, and true. Just like my Brendan. He was tough, and nothing irked him more than someone who wasn't living up to their potential or who refused to take responsibility for their actions. If I want to make him proud, I will live by those words every day.

I was honored to be the wife of Brendan Looney, if only for a short time. It was the greatest gift he could have given me. Every day, I hope that I can honor and respect him the way he honored and respected me. I want to be worthy to carry on his name and continue his legacy of strength and perseverance. This book is my attempt to do that, and it comes with some hard-fought battles and some harshly learned lessons.

At the end of the day, I choose to believe what Brendan told me about myself: that I am stronger than I know. I am able to say that with certainty today, only because I've waded through the fog of uncertainty. At different times during my journey of grief, I've been plagued with self-doubt and an endless stream of disorienting questions. In the end, however, there was always one question I came back to, and it taught me one of the most important lessons of my life.

CHAPTER 5

★ ★ ★

When "What If?" Becomes "What Now?"

I stood in my bedroom, staring quizzically at the inside of an empty hiking bag. I had no idea how to pack. At the foot of my bed lay two piles: one a "Definitely Bring," and the other a "Maybe Bring."

In the Definite category, so far, I had two sets of thick, woolen socks and a never-worn pair of the most heavy-duty hiking boots I could find at REI.

Everything else had been relegated to the Maybes. The Maybe heap was an eclectic combination of my belongings that rarely got to mix with one another: bathing suits tangled up in snow hats, and a bottle of sunscreen buried under a raincoat. I considered a series of possible outcomes for the trip ahead: *What if it pours buckets the whole time we're climbing the mountain? What if it's sweltering hot at the base of the mountain and biting cold at the top? What if one of the other women forgets to pack something?* I figured I'd just bring extras of everything and cover all my bases.

It had been four years since Brendan died, and I was about to embark on a week in the mountains of Peru with about a dozen other widows around my age who had also lost their husbands in service. And I wasn't just attending this expedition; I was leading it. It was both terrifying and exhilarating, particularly for someone like me, who had little experience with the wild outdoors.

If only Brendan could have seen me now. I have no doubt he'd wonder what happened to his Starbucks-latte-drinking wife and who was this other woman who was rummaging through her closet. I was preparing to hike a stretch of a fourteen-thousand-foot mountain with women as inexperienced as I, and the help of some very patient and savvy guides.

I had left my job in medical sales and taken a position with the Travis Manion Foundation, the organization created after the death of Brendan's best friend. I never dreamed that I'd be a staff member myself at the foundation one day, let alone leading the programs that support people just like me—families of the fallen.

I looked back at my "Maybe" pile and resolved to

dump the whole tower of clothes into my pack. Better to be safe than sorry, right? A million different things could happen on this hike—from weather extremes to injuries—and I wanted to be prepared for every one of them. I'd just about made up my mind on this packing strategy when I remembered the sage advice of an outdoorsy friend:

"What if?" weighs a lot.

Hmm…good point. Prior to remembering that advice, I'd been thinking, *What if it snows?* I'd toss a pair of gloves in my pack. *What if the terrain is rocky?* Better bring the hiking poles. I could practically feel my shoulders getting crushed under the weight of an increasingly heavy pack.

Extra weight was something I could not afford. I could imagine "What if?" scenarios until I was blue in the face. But the fact remained that each item would result in a heavier pack and a less pleasant experience. That lightweight raincoat *might* get used, but it might not. And it wasn't going to feel so "lightweight" three hours into a strenuous climb. Clearly, I needed to rethink my approach.

Over the years, I've had a fraught relationship with that question, "What if?"

I am a planner. Ryan and I could not be more different in this regard. Take, for example, the way we approached an interview we recently did together on *CBS This Morning.* I and my fellow authors, Ryan and

Heather, had been invited to the studio to share our stories of loss and grief.

I'd been interviewed about Brendan before, but never on a national outlet, where millions of people would be watching and listening.

Heather would be opening up for the first time publicly about losing her husband, Marine First Lieutenant Rob Kelly. Her father-in-law, General John Kelly, was serving as President Trump's White House chief of staff at the time, which only increased the segment's viewership and added to my fears. The night before the interview, Heather and I had experienced what I believe was a healthy dose of terror, and we wanted to prepare everything we could. Ryan, on the other hand, wanted nothing to do with it.

I had asked the producers to give us a set of questions that would resemble what we might be asked. I tend to get emotional when questioned about Brendan and I hoped that, by preparing well for the questions, I would be able to control those emotions.

The night before, I worked rigorously through the questions and prompts. In my head, I outlined, drafted, revised, and rehearsed each one, never feeling fully satisfied with my answers. I didn't want to sound scripted, but I needed to have my talking points solid before I could feel comfortable or satisfied.

I tried to get Ryan in on the process so we could approach the questions together. She immediately plugged her ears when I read the first question aloud. "Nope, don't tell me," she chided. "I don't want to hear them. Preparing for anything like this screws me up. The best way for me to prep is to watch TV and relax."

"What? How is that even possible?" I couldn't believe it. "I don't know how you operate like that. If I didn't prepare everything I did, I would get nothing done."

This, of course, was coming from a woman who rehearses everything from the questions I want to ask at my doctor's appointments, to the speeches I plan to give my credit card company when I see unfamiliar charges to my account. Before that interview, I considered every possible nightmare that could arise while I was talking: What if I lose my mind and mispronounce Brendan's name? What if I clam up before I can successfully get my message out? Or worse, what if I break down and can't finish my thought? Even my contingency plans have contingency plans. For me, "What if?" isn't some casual question I muse over when I'm feeling reflective. It's the strategy I've always depended on to feel prepared and to be successful.

There are some things, of course, that you simply can't prepare for, even if you're bold enough to imagine the nightmare scenarios. Yes, I had distantly and reluctantly considered that the death of my husband in Afghanistan while he was deployed was a real possibility. But there was no reasonable solution to that "What if?" scenario, so I shoved it away and tried not to think about it.

Now that it's become my reality, I am forced to think about it. Having Brendan in my life for only eight years was never the plan. Every day since September 21, 2010, I've been asking myself "What if?" What if he hadn't gone out that day? What if he had actually come home? What if it was just an injury he sustained and not death? And I'll tell you what: Asking that question has taught me something. My friend was right.

"What if?" weighs *a lot*.

There have been times when I've felt crushed under the weight of this question. My life could have been so different, I used to think. I'd have my husband, a beautiful family, and the life I had always imagined for myself. I felt cheated and bitter. But after years of asking this question, I've arrived at some surprising conclusions that have allowed me to imagine a better life for myself.

In order to share them, I have to go back to the beginning.

Brendan and I met at the Greene Turtle Sports Bar & Grille, in Baltimore, Maryland. We were both juniors in college, he at the United States Naval Academy in Annapolis, where he roomed with Travis Manion, and I at Johns Hopkins University, where I was studying business. It was Memorial Day weekend of 2003 and we nearly missed one another.

Brendan hadn't planned to go to the bar that night. He had been visiting friends for the long weekend at the Jersey Shore and had initially planned to stay at the beach through that Monday. But a group of his high school friends persuaded him to head back to Maryland and go out Sunday night. Fortunately for me, they must have made a strong case.

Brendan was a graduate of DeMatha Catholic High School, a prestigious, all-boys prep school outside Washington, where he was a competitive athlete and an impressive student. I can imagine right about now you're picturing a self-absorbed, entitled snob with a big ego, but I promise you, Brendan Looney was anything but. Nothing was ever handed to Brendan; he truly earned any accolade he ever received. Every day, he got up well before sunrise so he could drive the hour-long commute to the high school.

Even back then, he was responsible and hardworking. He was the oldest of six children and was used to playing the roles of leader and adviser. His family was tight-knit, loving, and practical. They didn't live a luxurious lifestyle, but what they did have went a long way. Like others in his family, Brendan was equal parts pragmatic and generous. He was mild-mannered and kind, but also tough. He was the most disciplined twenty-two-year-old I'd ever met.

But before I knew all that, he was just a cute boy at the Greene Turtle on the Sunday before Memorial Day. And that night, he was downright shy.

I, too, had gone to the bar with a friend from high

school, and she knew Brendan's DeMatha buddies from years before. Pretty soon, our groups were mingling. I could tell he wanted to talk to me, but he was more reserved than most, and he didn't quite seem to know how.

I decided to help him along a bit. We spent the rest of the night bar-hopping, flirting, and playing little cat-and-mouse games with one another until, at the end of the night, he finally worked up the courage to ask for my number.

I don't know where this is going to go, I thought to myself later that night. *Maybe he'll call and we'll go on a date, maybe not.*

Having grown up in the Annapolis area, I was familiar with the Naval Academy and its graduates. Was I even interested in dating someone in the Navy? Weren't they gone all the time? Fortunately, these questions felt like they concerned events far in the future and didn't deter me from enjoying the excitement of meeting someone new.

A couple of days went by and I hadn't heard a peep from Brendan. Initially, I thought I didn't care if I ever did, but as time went on, I realized I was actually very annoyed. We had a good time, didn't we? I couldn't have been the only one who felt that way. What happened?

Brendan was mature, but he was twenty-two just the same. As I later learned, he took his dating cues from

Vince Vaughn in the 1996 comedy *Swingers*: Waiting two days to call a girl is "industry standard," but waiting three days—"now, that's money." Brendan was probably surprised, then, on day three, when the first thing out of my mouth as I picked up the phone was, "It took you three days to finally call, huh?"

It's definitely not my personality to be so brazen, but at this point, I figured this wasn't going anywhere anyway. The stakes were pretty low, so I could be bold.

In fact, I almost didn't go out with him when he finally did ask me. But thankfully, I did end up accepting his invitation, and by the time we sat down at our table at Ruby Tuesday that evening, my attitude had changed entirely.

Our conversation was effortless and our connection instant. Brendan was sweet, respectful, and charming. He asked me about my family and told me all about his. He shared his goals and plans and I immediately got the sense that I fit into them.

He was very clear about his values and priorities, and I knew this guy was playing for keeps. What I didn't know, however, was that I was vying for the role of "girlfriend" against some fairly stiff competition.

Brendan had been casually dating another girl at the time he asked me out and had just taken her to his junior ring dance at the academy. Little did I know, he was deciding whether to get serious with her, and had asked me out just to see what else was out there. By the end of our date, I guess he'd made up his mind. And so had I.

From then on, we were inseparable. Or as inseparable as two college kids can be, when one is a collegiate athlete under the strict authority of service academy rules, and the other is a thirty-minute drive away.

And though that first year was a little difficult to balance, Brendan always found time for me. Even if it was just a few hours on a weeknight before he had to rush back for a room inspection. The days we didn't spend together in person, we'd spend together on the phone. We discussed everything: our family histories and what we wanted when we started our own families one day, our careers, our friends, our pet peeves, our goals, and our fears.

Even though things, initially, were easy and care-free between us, they got serious pretty quickly. There was no waiting period to "feel things out" or "see how it goes." With Brendan's demanding school and sports schedules, that wasn't an option anyway. Either we were doing this, or we weren't.

Within a couple of months, Brendan had come a long way from the reserved, shy boy I had met at the Greene Turtle. He was never the type to speak just to hear himself talk. He was far too humble for that. If he spoke, it was because he had something to say. During those months, he had a lot to say, and I loved hearing it.

Looking back, I realize it was probably not your typical

early-twenties relationship. The challenges posed by our schedules taught me early on that I would need to be independent, and Brendan's constant orientation toward the future made things pretty serious right off the bat.

There was very little gray area when it came to Brendan's intentions for me. And as a planner, that's just the way I liked it. Military life, on the other hand, was *all* gray area. I had had no experience with it, other than a grandfather who had served in World War II, which meant I had a lot to learn.

During one of our long phone conversations, Brendan shared with me that he had put in to become an Intelligence officer after graduation and a commissioned officer in the Navy. His dream was to be in the special warfare community as a Navy SEAL, but the fact that he was color-blind made that almost impossible. Intelligence was a good alternative, but in Brendan's mind, he still couldn't help wondering if there was something else out there for him.

"Okay, so you're doing Intel. What does that mean then?" I asked him one night. At that point there was still so much I didn't understand. To me, the military was a series of emblems and acronyms, and I was more interested in brass tacks.

"Well," he explained, "I'll have to go to more schooling in Virginia Beach. That's where all the Intel officers go after graduation."

"For how long?" I could feel myself getting defensive.

"I'm not sure. Maybe a year."

"Well, I'm in Maryland, Brendan." I was happy for him, of course. But I was graduating college and would be early on in my career, too. I needed to establish some footing. "I can't just uproot my life and move to be with you. My life is here."

"Amy, it's fine." He was even-keeled and calm by nature, but even more so when my anxieties were mounting. "Don't worry. We'll figure it out."

We did the best we could, but the distance certainly didn't make things any easier. We took turns driving the four hours between Virginia Beach and Columbia, Maryland, to see one another on weekends and we continued to make the most of our phone conversations.

At one point, almost a year into our relationship, I began to wonder if I'd made a mistake. I wasn't cut out for the military life, I decided: living at the mercy of the Navy's demands and always being forced to surrender your will to the powers that be.

I wanted to be with someone who was actually around and with whom I could spend time. Brendan was always doing things to woo and impress me, and while I loved it in one way, I also wondered if relationships were supposed to be more of a game or challenge. Besides, I was still young and this felt very serious. Had I really kissed all the frogs I needed to kiss in order to get to Prince Charming?

Before Brendan, I'd always gone for the bad boys: the charming, winsome partiers who adore the spotlight, thrive on attention, and rarely take notice of other people's feelings. And Brendan was the complete opposite. Here was a guy who, early in our relationship, asked me on a "date" to take our younger sisters to an ice show and bought them ice cream and souvenirs.

He was too disciplined an athlete to be a heavy drinker and too humble to command the center of attention. But still, I wondered if I was missing something, and Navy life was hard. I told Brendan I was sorry, but I couldn't do it anymore. We broke up.

And that lasted all of a week.

At some point during those seven days, I had the good sense to realize that, hey, maybe dating a good person was actually a good thing. Maybe spending my time with someone I genuinely admired, and who respected me in a way I deserved, was a rare blessing I might not get a shot at again, even if he did have a demanding career. I realized that having something real, authentic, and lasting was more important and enjoyable than the chase I'd grown accustomed to. Who knew?

Fortunately, it wasn't too difficult to persuade him to take me back. And after that, I jumped in with both feet. It was a good thing I did, because Brendan had his first deployment coming up—a full year in Korea— which was about to test our mettle.

It proved to be a long, lonely year without Brendan's calming presence in my life, but he was largely out of danger and, in the end, it only strengthened our commitment to one another.

But when he returned to Virginia Beach at the end of the deployment, he learned he would be deploying to Iraq a few months later. I was crushed. The next deployment would be only three months long, but it was about to take our lives in a very different direction.

Brendan deployed to Iraq in 2006, when things in the Middle East were very lively. While there, he continued to work in Intelligence, gathering and interpreting data about potential enemy threats and delivering it to the people responsible for responding to them.

Brendan was happy to be serving his country in a meaningful way, but it wasn't quite checking the box for him.

During his Iraq deployment, Brendan worked closely with a team of Navy SEALs, and he ached to be with them at the tip of the spear, knocking down doors and hunting down bad guys. He was excited, then, when he learned that changes in the restrictions around color blindness meant he could do a lateral transfer and compete for a spot on a SEAL team.

He still had to do the training, though, and there were no guarantees. He knew that only a small fraction of the guys who start BUD/S make it through to qualify as SEALs. Friends and colleagues advised him not to get his hopes up. But all Brendan heard was that the restriction had been lifted; the rest fell on deaf ears because his mind was already made up.

"I've put in my package to go to BUD/S," he told me when he got home. "And I really hope you'll support me."

I braced myself for an even longer-distance relationship. Training took place in California, and Brendan would be driving cross-country with his brother to start with BUD/S Class 265 in March 2007. What could I say? I would never feel right knowing I had held him back from his dream. And I was too naive at the time to truly understand the danger he was putting himself in. I had a vague sense that the Special Operations track he was starting on came with heightened risks, but the concepts of war, combat, and loss were still quite distant to me.

Until one month later, on April 29, 2007, when our lives took yet another jolting turn. That's when Brendan learned that his best friend and Naval Academy roommate, Travis Manion, had been killed in Iraq.

The news triggered something deep inside Brendan that changed him forever. He was devastated. But he could not even attend the funeral. Had he left his training, he would not have been allowed to return. He struggled with the guilt of not being able to be there to help lay Travis to rest on the East Coast or support his family in their greatest time of need. At twenty-six, he was on a career track that he had fought long and hard to join. But when his best friend died, Brendan took a hard look at his life and wondered if he was spending it the way he should be.

"I don't know, Amy," he told me on the phone one night. "Am I really doing all I can? I think about Travis and I just..." He paused, searching for his thoughts. "I just want to be living a life I can be proud of."

Death has a way of making those of us who survive question our life decisions. Initially, it throws us into a deep pit of doubt, but it also gives us a chance for reflection that we may not otherwise have. We think of the one we lost and immediately review our own life as though it, too, has passed.

We look at the relationships we've formed and the milestones we've hit, and we assess them with the grades we believe they've earned. The difference is, we have the ability to make choices that will alter our futures in a way that the people we mourn do not. When Brendan went through this exercise in 2007, he reached two conclusions:

First, he was on the right track in his career. He was going to throw himself into his new training and would dedicate every exhausting run in the sand, every cold, sleepless night, and every ache in his muscles to his friend Travis. There was no doubt in his mind that, very soon, he would be a Navy SEAL. And very soon after that, he would join the fight. No more waiting on the sidelines, as he felt he'd done in his two previous deployments. He wanted a direct shot at the forces of evil that threatened the American way of life and robbed us of good guys like Travis.

But second, he was still missing something critical before he could feel like his life's mission was complete. That was what he told me when I traveled to visit him in California in June 2007, following his completion of the first phase of the six-month BUD/S program. We had just finished eating at George's at the Cove, a fancy restaurant in La Jolla, where we had toasted the end of Brendan's initial round of SEAL training.

"So, you graduated Hell Week."* I smiled at him and held my glass of champagne aloft. "Now what?"

"I don't know. I guess we'll see what the Navy has in mind."

I felt a gray cloud of "What ifs?" looming over our table. *What if we have to continue this long-distance relationship? We can't keep this up forever. What if he has to deploy immediately? What if we can't make this work?* I tried to initiate a serious conversation about where we were headed, but Brendan's thoughts were elsewhere. I was ready to plan my future, but it was awfully hard, not to

---

* Hell Week is the nickname for the final five days of the first phase of SEAL training, or BUD/S. SEAL hopefuls are forced to train for several days with little sleep, in nonstop evolutions of difficult physical feats and psychological tests. They brave icy temperatures, carry heavy gear and equipment, and receive no more than five hours of sleep during the five days.

mention frustrating, with so many variables in my way. Every question I posed ended at the same dead-end response.

"I don't know, Amy," he said with some finality. "We'll see."

Okay, that was it. I had just flown all the way across the country to celebrate with him and he'd been acting like a weirdo all night. I was at my absolute wits' end trying to keep things together. I'd been as patient with this chaotic schedule and our limited communication as I could possibly be. I'd endured two deployments, one a full year long, and was bracing myself for another set of deployments on the horizon with the SEAL teams. I had had enough.

"You know what? I'm just going to get a flight home in the morning," I shot back.

Brendan suggested we take a walk by the beach to cool off.

"I don't need to cool off. And I'm in a dress and heels. I'm not really interested in a walk right now."

"Ten minutes, Amy? That's all I'm asking."

"Fine."

As we walked along the San Diego shoreline, I began to understand why Brendan had been acting so strangely. He shared how deeply affected he was by Travis's death only a couple months before, and I felt guilty for not having been more sensitive to his feelings. He was such a tough guy, I saw him as invincible. It was easy to forget that he was also very sensitive and that he felt things so deeply.

"I just can't stop thinking about him," he told me. "I just never thought it would be Trav, you know? I had a care package sitting on my kitchen counter that I never even got to mail to him."

I gripped his hand a little tighter as we walked but didn't say anything in response.

"There was still so much he had left to do, too. He would have had such an awesome career in the Marines. He would have been such a good dad, a great husband. He never got any of that. He never got the chance to have what we have. He didn't have anyone that he wanted to spend his life with."

We had stopped walking and Brendan turned to face me. I realized that it had been a long time since I'd seen him dressed in anything but lacrosse shorts and flip-flops. Did he have to borrow that button-down from a friend? It didn't look familiar.

"Amy, Travis didn't have anyone he wanted to live out his days or have adventures with, but I do. It's got me thinking." He started to fumble around looking for something in his pocket.

"Life is short. I know this hasn't been easy on you, and I can't promise that things will get any easier from here. I just couldn't imagine a life for me that doesn't have you in it. I want you to live here. I don't want roommates anymore and I don't want long distance. I just want us to start our lives together. I love you." He was down on one knee now.

"Will you marry me?"

I was shocked. I was also very embarrassed about the hard time I'd been giving him only minutes before. Man, did I feel like a jerk. But more than anything, I was ecstatic.

"Of course!"

We chose July 12, 2008, for our wedding date in Annapolis, which gave us a little more than a year to plan. It was a perfect time line, because Brendan had been given the heads-up from his leadership that he would likely be assigned to SEAL Team Five, which wasn't slated to deploy until October. That gave us a full three months to enjoy just being newlyweds in Southern California. And believe it or not, that felt like an eternity. Once again, however, we'd have another curveball to handle.

At the last minute, in May 2008, Brendan was reassigned to SEAL Team Three and—surprise—was required to deploy immediately.

"Wait, what?" I stared at him blankly when he told me the news. "Brendan, we have a church, a DJ, invitations out, and 250-odd people who think they're coming to our wedding in July. And you're telling me you're not even going to be there?"

"I'll fix this," Brendan assured me. Sometimes he was so calm it was irksome.

But he was also a man of his word. On Saturday, July 12, 2008, in front of all of our friends and family, I became Mrs. Brendan Looney. And two days later, on Monday July 14, my groom was gone again. He remained assigned to Team Three, and the ink was barely dry on our marriage certificate before he rushed off immediately after our wedding to meet the rest of his platoon on deployment in Iraq.

Brendan returned home in October, and we were both grateful that it had been a shorter deployment for him since he had joined it so late. But that temporary victory was soon followed by a permanent loss. For it was his next deployment—to Afghanistan—that claimed his life. If only he had been assigned to Team Five as we had expected, things might have been different. Sure, he'd have had a longer deployment that first time around, but he might also still be here today.

I still have the accident report from Brendan's death filed away. I can't bring myself to read what happened to him and his friends in their final moments. When I look back on the eight years that Brendan and I had together, I'm struck by all the close shaves we had. We *almost* had a shot at a different life.

"What if?" weighs a lot.

What if Brendan had stayed in Intelligence? What if they had never lifted the restrictions on color blindness that allowed him to join the SEALs? What if he had never been moved to Team Three? What if he hadn't gone out on that fifty-ninth, final combat mission, which ultimately ended his life? What if he had stayed behind, or had been given some other responsibility? Would my husband still be here? What if he could have avoided danger for *just a few more weeks*? That's all he would have needed in order to come home to me.

It's a dangerous game to play, as you can imagine. And I've played it more times than I can count. But in the years since I lost Brendan, I've learned that there's a secret rule to the "What if?" game that very few people know about.

It's a two-way street.

People tend to forget that. You can't simply imagine the thousands of tiny, lamentable decisions that made your life go wrong without also considering the millions of fortuitous choices you made that caused your life to go right. I thought I'd stay Mrs. Brendan Looney forever. And yes, maybe I *almost* did. But I also *almost* never met the man who changed me forever. We almost never dated. We almost never married. I almost missed out on one of the greatest blessings of my life. So let's roll the tape back, and try the "What if?" game again:

What if Brendan had never driven down from the Jersey Shore that Memorial Day Sunday to meet his friends (and me!) at the Greene Turtle? After all, he almost didn't. What if Brendan hadn't rolled the dice on me and had opted instead for his junior ring date partner? After all, he almost hadn't. What if I had decided that military life was too hard? That I was missing out on someone better when I felt lonely and frustrated waiting for Brendan to come home? After all, I almost did.

What a gift I would have missed.

"What if?" can be a deeply heavy and burdensome question. It will crush us, if we let it.

But if we accept the weight that that question heaves on our shoulders, we can become stronger in the process. In order to do so, we must discover gratitude. We must find perspective.

That's what I learned in the mountains of Peru, surrounded by women like me. There are a lot of us out there, you know. We've all lost someone we loved deeply—a boyfriend, a fiancé, a husband—to a war thousands of miles away that we only partially understand.

We've known the joys of finding that one person in the world with whom we wanted to create a home and plan a future. And we've known the heartache of losing it all in a single, unexpected moment. But most important, we've all had that same burning, two-word question weighing on our minds and testing our emotional strength at one point or another.

Over the course of the weeklong expedition, we conquered the literal and figurative mountain in front of us. We worked up a sweat together, we slept in tents together, we ate terrible, pre-packaged food together, and we shared our most painful and joyous memories with one another. And somewhere along the route, as we wearily moved from checkpoint to checkpoint, our burdens—and our spirits—lifted.

Some of these women had been strangers to me at the base of the mountain. But right around day three, just as I was tired and dirty enough to not bother mounting some defense that made me seem more okay than I really was, I found myself sharing things with them that I hadn't shared with anyone else.

And they got it. I told them that I felt robbed and cheated and angry, and they nodded in agreement. I told them how I was sick of being the constant third wheel at dinner with my couple friends; that I was so over hearing my girlfriends complain about their spouses— who actually get to come home to them each night after work. I told them about my struggles with "What if?" and my occasional thoughts that my suffering was meaningless and might have been avoided. I wondered if this was all for nothing. It was affirming to know that I wasn't alone and that many of them felt the same way and wondered the same things.

And then, on the final day of our climb, we reached the top. We stood together and watched a golden sunset drip down past the peak of the mountain that we had just worked so hard to summit. I was simultaneously physically drained and emotionally refreshed. I was filled to the brim with gratitude and awe. I gave thanks for my strong body, which had carried me up; for my even stronger mind, which had pushed me through some difficult times; and for the friendship of some of the strongest women I'd ever had the great fortune to stand beside. In that moment, my doubts dissolved. I knew the suffering couldn't all be for nothing.

It's worth noting that my packing job proved to be a disaster. By no means did I have all the equipment or supplies to deal with all the unexpected incidents that happened along the route. But who knows? What if I had? I might not have made it up the mountain. My pack was light(ish) and I had the bare essentials. In the end, that's exactly what I needed to succeed. We may think we need more to overcome struggles or to achieve our goals. But so much of it is already within us.

The woman Brendan left was a different woman than the one he had met just a few years before. He taught me humility and discipline. He taught me patience and grace. The relationships that we form and the experiences we endure will *always* change us. That is a fact.

I can promise you now that, if you haven't done so already, you too one day will know the feeling of a heavy burden on your shoulders. You too will carry the load of "What if?" It will weigh you down for a bit, and that's to be expected. Just make sure it doesn't crush you. Allow it to make you stronger. When you're in the midst of your own struggle, it's hard to believe this is possible. But it is.

"I KNOW THIS WON'T MAKE SENSE TO YOU RIGHT
NOW, BUT I PROMISE YOU, YOU WILL BE OKAY."

This was the most helpful comment I received from anyone throughout my entire grieving process, and it came from a woman I barely knew. I wanted to roll my eyes when she said it. The Navy had connected me with Char, now a dear friend of mine, who had lost her husband five years before I lost Brendan.

It was a nice gesture to remind me that life goes on. I nodded and smiled politely at her words, but I wasn't buying them. *What does she know?* I thought. *She's remarried and starting a new family. She can't possibly understand.*

I was wrong. Sometimes you're too absorbed in your own struggle to imagine that there could ever be a life outside it. But there is. And it's a good life at that. Just as I didn't believe Char, you may not believe me when I tell you that. And I can't say I would blame you if you don't. But if you can give up any of your doubt, give it up to the possibility that life gets better.

Grief may cause you to stop believing in a lot of things: a benevolent God, a life plan, the goodness of other people. But you must always believe in possibility. It can be tempting to shut down and close yourself off completely. Don't do it. Leave the door open, if only a crack.

THE PATH TO GRATITUDE LIES IN OPENNESS.

This is why it's so important to leave that door open to possibility. Discovering gratitude will help you find happiness once again. I would love to advise you to take notice of the many blessings in your life even when it feels like your world is crumbling around you. I would love to remind you to relish the good stuff of life, since that is what will bring you the joy you may be lacking— and that you so deserve. I believe that's all true. But I know it is a lot easier said than done. So at the risk of sounding Pollyanna-ish, I won't tell you to be grateful. I'll tell you to be *open*. And I'll trust that gratitude will find you along the way.

If you have ever experienced loss—whether the loss of a relationship, a career, or a loved one—you know that the void left behind isn't easily filled. The role Brendan played in my life will never be replaced. But the gap that his absence left in my life has made me a more open person. I'm open to understanding the trials of others and listening to them with patience and empathy. I'm open to climbing mountains with strangers in order to learn more about myself. I'm open to embracing new and scary challenges, like the challenge of sharing my deepest and most painful experiences with strangers in a book that no one may read.

In each of these experiences, when I start with an open heart, I end with a grateful one. You have to experience the extreme fatigue, muscle aches, and frustration that come with climbing a mountain to appreciate the sunset at the top. Your suffering has the power to make you a more grateful—and therefore happier—person. Let it.

If, however, you have not experienced the kind of grief and struggle that help you connect with the pain of others, you may be on a different path right now. That's okay, too. In fact, it's great. Rather than stand idly by, you've decided to choose the road of empathy and you try to better identify with something or someone outside yourself. As you do so, let me caution you:

DON'T CONFUSE EMPATHY WITH PITY.

People ask me if I believe Brendan's death "was meant to be." Honestly, I have no idea. I'm not even sure I know what "meant to be" means. What I do know is that, if Brendan had to die at so young an age and with so healthy a mind and body, this is how he would have wanted it to happen—in service to his country. Now, it's not how I wanted it to happen, but I know he could have imagined no greater honor.

He knew what he had signed up for and he believed passionately in his mission and cause. And while I could be naive at times, I too knew what he had signed up for. Please, do not pity me. Over the years since Brendan was killed, I've had the great fortune to get to know hundreds of families of the fallen. No matter how many encounters I have with our Gold Star families,[*] I am always awed by the poise and strength they exhibit.

We may be tempted to sympathize with these families, to treat them like charity cases. This is a well-intentioned impulse, but it's a misdirected one. To pity our Gold Star families would be to do them a great disservice. They are far stronger than most realize, and they can teach the rest of us a great deal. The most valuable lessons I've learned have come from the men and women who have gone before me, and who have grown from the grief that they may have believed, at one point, would ruin them. Get to know them. Learn their stories and the stories of their loved ones. You may be surprised at what you find.

---

[*] *Gold Star families* refers to those who have lost a loved one who served our country.

★ ★ ★

Preparing for the Unknown

I have a photo that captures Brendan perfectly. It was taken on deployment, somewhere in the deserts of Iraq or the mountains of Afghanistan. I'm not sure if he was aware of the photographer's presence at the time, since it's more of a profile shot. It shows him crouched close to the ground against an empty and mountainous terrain, looking into the distance with just the faintest of smiles, one that's equal parts mischief and warmth. He's wearing full camo, probably forty-plus pounds of gear, sporting a heavy and untamed beard typical of those worn by men in that region of the world, and holding a sniper rifle close to his chest. He is staring at the landscape, ready to take on whatever may be in his path. It's Brendan just as I remember him: young, strong, calm, and prepared for whatever life is about to throw at him. It's also the quintessential "tough guy" military photo, and if I didn't know any better, I would guess it was staged for a Navy SEAL recruitment poster.

Except for one little detail that you could miss at first.

If you look closely at the image, you see that Brendan is not alone. Popping its head out of a satchel attached to Brendan's hip is a tiny gray puppy. The little guy looks to be only days old. His eyes are closed and he is stretching his neck just barely out of the satchel toward the warm sun. He looks so vulnerable and sweet that, once you spot him, you wonder how you could have ever missed him. The soft, innocent puppy creates quite the contrast next to Brendan in his desert cammies.

Brendan was a complex guy, and I'm sure no number of pages I write could really do his character justice, but that picture tells you just about everything you need to know about him. He was a rugged warrior, no doubt, but once you got to know him, you discovered that he was also a sensitive soul who couldn't resist scooping up a puppy that looked like it needed safekeeping.

He was a protector, and after that day, that pup became his constant companion on deployment. Above all else, that photo reminds me of two principles that Brendan never spoke out loud, but that he lived by every day: Be prepared and be present. He was ready to do battle with any challenge and would work tirelessly to conquer it. But he was not so focused on the failings of the past or the ambitions of the future to pass over the simple, sweet gifts of the present.

When I reflect on my late husband and the growth I've experienced in the years since I lost him, I always return to these two lessons. First and foremost, Brendan taught me preparation. Unbeknownst to him—or me, at the time—Brendan prepared me for the life I would have with him. He prepared me to be Mrs. Amy Looney.

Before Brendan, I had lived a sheltered, and at times unstable, life. I began my life in Delaware, and my parents divorced when I was four.

I spent a lot of time alone and learned early on that, if I wanted something to be done, I was going to have to figure out how to do it myself. I spent most of my early years with my grandparents, with whom I became very close. With them, I felt safe and at home, insulated from the world in a protective bubble.

When I was thirteen, my mom and I uprooted, leaving my grandparents and moving to Maryland, where she remarried. That relationship also ended in divorce, and my mom wound up working long, difficult hours to support our family on her own.

For me, the move away from my grandparents was also difficult. I felt like my familiar life had been ripped from me and I was being forced to start over and try to create some sense of stability on my own.

I ultimately adjusted. I stayed in Maryland through college, and never dreamed of leaving that fifty-mile radius of home, which was now predictable, pleasant, and stable.

My upbringing had taught me to be independent, but I'd also grown accustomed to a quiet family life. When it came to relationships, I planned to stay young and single for as long as I could, until I was 300 percent sure that I was ready to commit to something that wouldn't fall apart. Maybe when I was thirty.

And then, of course, I met Brendan. Plans went out the window pretty quickly. Rather than staying in my insulated hometown, I moved across the country to a new life, a new job, and new friends, to marry a man whose career was neither predictable nor stable.

"I don't know if I can do this," I remember admitting to Brendan shortly after we became engaged. I was worried about starting out at ground zero with a new career and having to settle for some job I wasn't happy with, just to have a steady income.

"That's ridiculous," he responded. "Of course you can do this. You can do anything."

Brendan wasn't saying that just to make me feel better or to be dismissive of my concerns. He really believed it. Sometimes he was so persuasive that he got me to believe it, too. With his certainty uplifting me, suddenly jet-setting to the West Coast proved to be more exciting than terrifying.

And when I met the Looney family, I found that any ideas I had had about a quiet, simple family life also disappeared. That house was straight-up organized chaos, yet somehow I felt at home in it. I'd never been around so many distinct, vivacious personalities at one time. And they all got along with one another to boot. This was unfamiliar territory for sure. They celebrated everything. At every uncle's birthday, every cousin's baptism, every going away or welcoming home, there was a party. It was a far cry from the quiet holiday dinners I was used to having with just my mom, my sister, and myself.

At first, it was overwhelming, but eventually I loved seeing Brendan in his family role playing the part of the dependable leader and trustworthy confidant to anyone with a problem. I remember thinking to myself, *This is what a family should be.*

As for my plan for staying young and single—well, I guess we know how that ended. At every stage, Brendan had a way of inadvertently forcing me to challenge my own beliefs—about values, about family, about my future, and most especially about myself. He saw something within me that I simply couldn't see for myself. He saw my strength long before I knew it was there. "You're so much stronger than you think you are," he would always say.

This proved true, even in small, day-to-day ways. I remember him taking me to the beach one day and telling me, "Okay, now we're going to do wind sprints."

"Are you nuts? I can't do that." Exhausting workouts were a part of Brendan's day-to-day routine. I couldn't say the same for myself.

"Yes, you can, Amy. You can do this."

Brendan knew I wasn't much of a fitness junkie at the time, but he wasn't going to let me off easy, either. He rarely missed a workout, and on the few occasions that he did, it was for some equally noble commitment he'd made instead. And he would just beat himself up about missing a day in his fitness routine. *Okay, so you missed a workout*, I would think. *So what?* I never understood the big deal.

After enduring several years of Brendan pushing me to be stronger, braver, and more disciplined, I understand. Before Brendan, I was rarely self-motivated. I liked to try hard or perform well and be a decent student and worker, but none of those things defined my personality as they did for him. It was Brendan who pushed me outside my comfort zone; Brendan who challenged me to be better every day. And now I don't need that external push. He made me realize that everything I need is already within me.

It wasn't Brendan's nature to point out people's flaws simply for the heck of it, however, and when he challenged me to be better, I knew he had my best interests in mind. I never felt like I was being beaten down. On the contrary, he was lifting me up. He knew what I was capable of and he wanted me to know it, too.

Whether I *could* do wind sprints, or move across the country, or start a new career, was not the issue. That was a foregone conclusion in Brendan's mind. As my biggest advocate, he knew that I *could*. That wasn't the point. He was going to ensure that *I did*. And he was going to be there to support me every step of the way.

It's probably not surprising, then, that I truly believed my late husband was invincible. It's stupid and naive to think that now, after losing him, but I only ever knew him as the person who was in total control of any situation. He knew what to do at all times. He was smart, he was strong, he was trained. I was confident that, if something bad happened on deployment, he would have a plan to get everyone out safely.

I couldn't imagine a scenario where he was anything but calm, decisive, and competent. In our marriage, I relied on him when things seemed uncertain or the path ahead was murky, and I trusted his judgment implicitly. I know he loved that I depended on him so much, but it must have concerned him on some level as well.

When Brendan deployed on my twenty-ninth birthday in March 2010, that was the last time I saw him alive. Before he left, however, he wanted us to have a special day together. He was very thoughtful whenever it came to any celebration, and he'd spend weeks coming up with a theme for each birthday. In 2010, the theme was "self-sufficiency."

Brendan knew I had an expensive daily Starbucks habit, so he went out and got me a Nespresso machine and enough pods of coffee to keep it running through October, when he was scheduled to return home.

"And then, when I'm back," he told me proudly, "I'll make your lattes for you every day. But until then, you can save yourself the time and money, and make them here."

He then presented me with a Williams Sonoma Crock-Pot recipe book to encourage more eating in than going out. I'm no Susie Homemaker, but experimenting with that book gave me something fun to do while he was away, and now, years later, it has become frayed with use. Brendan put a lot of thought into what life would be like for me while he was away, and he wanted to know that I was being taken care of, even when he couldn't be there to do the caring himself.

I believe he considered the possibility, too, that I might be forced to take on life without him. And if that were to happen, he wanted me to know that I had the strength and ability to do it.

And of course, as always, he pushed me. He pushed me to learn, to grow, and to become a better version of myself every day. Constant personal improvement was deeply important to Brendan—so much so that, when he bombed a presentation at work one day, he came home and asked me to join Toastmasters with him. Bettering ourselves came to be one of the ways that we bonded profoundly, and it helped us to grow not just as individuals, but as a couple as well.

Brendan prepared me for marriage by promoting my personal growth and introducing me to the values that would anchor our relationship.

He prepared me for Navy life by empowering me to become adaptable, adventurous, and flexible in ways that I hadn't thought possible.

He prepared me for life as a leader and a professional by showing me that respect from others is what you earn when you show them you are in it with them; that you are right there, climbing the mountain and sweating, just as they are.

In watching Brendan grieve the loss of Travis, and seeing how he prioritized his life afterward, I discovered that he had prepared me to grieve, too. Neither of us could have known it at the time, but the most important thing my husband prepared me to do was to be his widow.

During the eight years I had with Brendan, he helped me build a foundation that I would be forced to fall back on, time and time again, when I felt alone, defeated, and hopeless. He had helped me to become resilient, patient, and gracious.

I believe Brendan was put in my life to teach me to be a survivor and to make something meaningful of my life after his death.

While the deep pain of losing him was unlike anything

I'd ever experienced before, I found comfort in the little victories of past struggles that I'd overcome. Each one was a reminder of a time when I thought I couldn't possibly do something, and Brendan had shown me that I could.

He taught me the value of perseverance and the necessity of discipline. When I wanted to stay in my pajamas all day and wallow on the couch, I couldn't, because I didn't want to let him down.

If I hadn't known my husband was watching me from somewhere, believe me, I would have stayed on that couch. When I wanted to retreat from the world and numb my pain with alcohol or sleeping pills, I'd catch myself and exercise some discipline, because I wanted to make him proud.

While I'm grateful for the values and habits he helped me cultivate, I can't say that having them has made losing Brendan any easier. Nothing could make that loss easier; there's no agony like it. But it did provide me with the confidence I needed to know that, in the end, I would be okay. "I'm so much stronger than I think I am," I've reminded myself over the years. Brendan knew it was true long before I did, and his encouragement has spurred me on these past several years.

Emboldened by this knowledge, I began to see just what I was capable of. I wasn't scared anymore. The worst thing I could ever have imagined had happened. What more could there possibly be to risk? That put things into perspective quickly. Pretty soon, the ambitions and feats that had once been too fearful to tackle didn't seem so frightening.

In the first five years after Brendan's death, I ran a marathon, hiked Machu Picchu, went white-water rafting, and trained to swim the English Channel as part of a relay group. I am neither a natural athlete nor an adventurist, so my ability to achieve these milestones had less to do with any skills or inclinations I possessed, and more to do with constant, disciplined, and often painful preparation.

It was a beautiful gift that Brendan gave me in making me Mrs. Amy Looney. I am forever indebted to him for the life he prepared me for, as both a wife and a survivor. That realization is comforting, but it's also deeply painful. How can you not question why someone was placed in your life at just the right time, only to be ripped from it before you got the chance to run your course together? Why were you prepared for a life that you will never get to enjoy fully?

Three years after Brendan died, on Christmas Day 2013, Brendan's brother and his wife, Ali, had a son, and I was fortunate enough to meet him shortly after he was born. They named him Brendan Travis, and to this day, that fearless little boy lives up to his warrior name. Sharing in that moment at the hospital was difficult because it was a sharp reminder of the life I would never have. Brendan's brother had always told me that he wanted me to find happiness, in whatever form that may take.

And as I have watched Brendan Travis grow, I have realized I wanted that, too. Finally, encouraged by the support of friends and family, I was able to admit that I was ready to love again.

At this point, I'd found that training in frigid open waters wasn't all that intimidating, and that hiking up to the clouds with inadequate gear and even less adequate training was quite manageable. But the idea of dating again, let alone finding someone to love? Now, that was downright terrifying. Where would I even begin?

I received a lot of unsolicited—and, frankly, unwanted—advice in those days: when would be the "acceptable" time to start dating; who would be "appropriate" candidates; and how and when I would be obligated to share my past.

Nothing, however, was quite as frustrating as divorced friends telling me they knew *exactly* how I felt. We were basically in the same situation, right? Wrong. We weren't. I had loved my husband with all my heart, and our relationship ended abruptly on terms neither of us had decided upon.

I was still frozen with fear that I didn't have any love left to give to another man and questioned if I could ever put myself back out there. Needless to say, the additional opinions from outsiders about how, when, where, and to what degree I ought to proceed with my love life made the situation that much more difficult to navigate.

Dating as a young widow is scary. If you've ever been in this situation and gone for it, I commend you. When all you've ever known is a happy and loving marriage, it's impossible to imagine that you can ever find such a thing again. Could that really come more than once in a lifetime? And even if you meet someone and things look promising, there are so many new fears to consider.

Yes, the regular self-doubt is there, too. You become hyperaware of the weird chewing habit that you've always had but that your husband was happy to overlook; or you all of a sudden decide some birthmark you have, which had never bothered you before, will be a total turnoff to someone else. But along with all the usual insecurities and self-criticisms, the fear of loving and losing again takes over.

Let's say you're crazy and brave enough to put yourself out there. Let's go outside the realm of what you imagine as likely, and say you meet someone amazing and things click effortlessly. Here is where you have a "What if?" field day: What if they cheat and break your heart? What if they decide they don't love you anymore? What if they die? By the time you get to that last question, a caring girlfriend gently tells you you're being paranoid and that you shouldn't overthink things. But you know better. You've lived it. You know how very real nightmares can become.

It's courageous to ask your wounded heart to love again, to make yourself vulnerable again. But you've made it this far, haven't you? I remembered Brendan's response on the beach during wind sprints and any other time I questioned myself: "You're brave, remember? You can do anything."

A year after meeting baby Brendan in the hospital, I met Joel. It was nothing like when I had met Brendan in my early twenties, with our whole lives lying before us. It was a setup from a mutual friend of Brendan's and mine. I walked into that date cautious and nervous, but also feeling that something was going to be different and special about this person. We met for drinks because, secretly, neither of us wanted to commit to a full night of dinner and forced conversation. If the evening proved to be a disaster, I could bail.

Fortunately, I didn't need to. Joel and I talked about everything from music, to life, to previous relationships, to work, to travel. It was by far one of the most in-depth and honest conversations I had had with a man in a very long time. For years, Joel had been a Marine himself, and he was now in a career dedicated to public service. He knew what it meant to be away from loved ones, to sacrifice, to lose. I think he was surprised and relieved to find that I understood those things, too.

That evening, Joel walked me back to my apartment complex and we parted ways. I had the biggest, most genuine smile on my face when he dropped me at my door. It was the best five hours I'd spent with anyone in a long time.

It was easy to like Joel. His thick Chicago accent is endearing, and he's quick to share his ever-present smile with anyone he meets. He lights up a room as soon as he enters it and displays a warm, welcoming, and friendly demeanor that makes you want to open up to him, even if you're the reluctant type, as I originally was.

What attracted me to Joel from the beginning was his ability to get to know people deeply and to try to learn everything he could about them. He really invests in others and takes the time needed to build strong relationships with them. He did this for every single one of my closest friends, making a genuine effort to get to know the people closest to me.

He's good at it. After meeting friends whom I've known for years, Joel will tell me things about them that I never knew. His questions are always intended to help him understand people better: what makes them tick, their perspective on various topics, and their views on life.

One thing I'll never forget about our early relationship was how Joel made me feel, even from the start: safe, secure, and known. Immediately, I felt loved in a way that I hadn't felt since Brendan died. He made every effort to make me feel whole again and has one of the biggest hearts of anyone I know. His capacity for love seems nearly endless. He'll do anything for someone he cares about, and he'll do it with an easygoing, light-hearted attitude.

Nothing rattles Joel. Like me, he's seen hardship, which allows us to connect with one another and gain perspective about what truly matters in life. At the end of the day, what matters most to us is each other. We each put the other first because we know how fortunate we are to be part of such a loving and powerful relationship.

Most important, Joel loves me for my past just as much as he loves me for my present. He respects my relationship with Brendan and asks thoughtful questions about him. Even early on, he was confident and comfortable enough in his own skin that he didn't feel as though he was being compared with anyone else.

It would be silly and wrong for me to compare my love for Joel to my love for Brendan. I swore I would never do that because I think that doing so would set up any couple for failure.

They are completely different relationships and neither one replaces the other. I'm a different person from the person I was nine years ago. My experiences have changed me. And they've changed me in such a way that I'm now the perfect fit for Joel, and he's the perfect fit for me. This wasn't and couldn't have been true nine years ago. I can honestly say that I love and cherish the life I have now, and that's because of Joel.

On October 14, 2017, three years after we met, Joel

and I married in his home city of Chicago. I was filled with excited nerves in the back of the venue as I waited to greet my new husband. Just before I prepared to walk down the aisle, the wedding coordinator guided our two little ring bearers in front of me. It was such a powerful moment, one that I'll always remember, because it made me stop and marvel at the journey my life had taken until that point.

Brendan Travis Looney, who was now four years old, walked down the aisle in his black tuxedo and Converse All Star shoes. He walked arm in arm with Travis Brendan Borek, Ryan Manion's three-year-old son. Travis Brendan and Brendan Travis, two little boys who bear the names of two great men they never got to meet. They were family now, and it was important to both Joel and me that they play a special role in our day. They represented new beginnings, old legacies, and a messy, beautiful life that I have come to love.

Brendan and Travis smiled radiantly as they approached my future husband. When they reached the altar, Joel reached down and gave them each a giant grin and a high five. I've never felt so fortunate. In that moment, I knew I'd found a life partner who loved me not in spite of my past, but because of it. Because he knows that my past is what made me the woman I am, the woman he was marrying that day, and the woman with whom he wanted to build a new future.

I'm so grateful for having found the courage to open

my heart again, and I'm grateful to have a husband who recognizes and values that courage. He tells me all the time how much he admires me for starting my life over at twenty-nine and opening myself up to love again. He commends me for not attempting to erase my past, but for embracing it and pushing forward.

He hates what I had to go through to get myself to this place, but he believes wholeheartedly that I am the person he loves today because of the challenges and obstacles I faced. He knows how much I value our love and relationship because I know what it is like to love deeply and then lose that love. He knows I will do everything in my power to make our marriage work.

And I admire him just as much. I admire that he was willing to date a young widow, even with all the uncomfortable and awkward moments that accompanied that decision. I'm so grateful to Joel for showing me that love still matters, that it still exists, and that there is still a beautiful life waiting for us.

There was a time when I simply didn't think that was an option. As Joel's best man said in his wedding toast, "It is a testament to the character that Joel and Amy have that so many of Brendan's friends, teammates, and family are in this room celebrating tonight."

He was right. My marriage with Brendan is still a very important part of who I am now, and the relationships that I formed when he was alive play an integral role in my life today. Joel has graciously accepted all of them because he knows that they are part of my identity, and that our marriage is all the stronger for them.

There are times when I think how lucky I've been to have two great loves of my life. There are other times when I think how unlucky I am to have two great loves of my life. I will always treasure the past, and the special life that Brendan and I created together. I still mourn the future I almost had, but today I love the present with all my heart.

In the end, the greatest thing Brendan prepared me for was the life I would have without him. He was the first person who taught me to love unconditionally. We vowed our lives to one another, in front of friends and family, on July 12, 2008, and I keep that promise today.

The love that Joel and I share is entirely different from the love that Brendan and I shared, and it is no less precious to me. It has been an amazing gift to know that I can be happy and fulfilled in a relationship that is separate from and incomparable to the life I led previously.

I'm forever indebted to Brendan for helping me to develop the resilience that would strengthen me to open my heart again; and to Joel for affirming that doing so would be worth it. He reminds me what love is and provides me with the kind of life I didn't think was possible for me.

The last decade or so has been quite the roller-coaster

ride. Is it the life I pictured for myself as a little girl? No, it is not. But whose is? Is *anyone* living the life they thought they would be living by this point? I doubt it. If nothing else, it has taught me some powerful lessons around expectations, reality, and love:

FIRST AND FOREMOST, CHOOSE COURAGE.

It's not the easier path of the two, that I can promise you. It's almost certainly far more difficult and painful. But it will bring you more joy and peace than you can possibly imagine. This is one beautiful, harsh life we're all leading, and we're going to get knocked around a time or two. After every fall, we have to be prepared to stand back up. After losing Brendan, opening myself up to love was the second hardest thing I'd ever had to do. And in truth, I didn't "have" to do it. I could have stayed on stable ground and lived a decent and possibly contented life.

If nothing else, I wouldn't have known what I was missing. But by the time I lost Brendan, I'd made a habit—largely due to Brendan—of being courageous and resilient. And every small victory along the way gave me just enough confidence to take another shot. If I could do wind sprints, I was tougher than I thought I was. If I was tougher than I thought I was, I could move to a new city. If I was brave enough to move to a new city, I was brave enough to start a new career. If I was brave enough to start a new career, I was strong enough to handle loss. If I could handle loss, I could handle anything. You don't need to have buried your husband to know that you have courage. You just need to have experienced defeat somewhere in your life. If you don't know what defeat feels like or you haven't found something to fail at yet, you're not trying enough new things.

SECOND, BUILDING A NEW PRESENT DOES NOT WHITEWASH YOUR PAST.

Life is complicated. It's fluid and dynamic, and as easy to grasp hold of as it is to nail Jell-O to a wall. Today you are wonderful and strong, and tomorrow you might be hopeless and scared. That's simply how it works. But if you're lucky enough to find the courage to build a new life for yourself after struggle, or you're fortunate enough to watch someone else do the same, know that the scars of the past don't simply disappear once you establish a new present. I can't tell you how many people wanted to dismiss the pain of losing Brendan after they learned that I'd started a new life with Joel. Remarriage doesn't eliminate the pain of widowhood. Recovery doesn't cancel the pain of illness or addiction. Healing doesn't remove the wounds of abuse. Finding joy in the present means accepting the difficulties of the past, not forgetting them.

FINALLY, YOU NEVER KNOW WHAT YOU'RE BEING PREPARED FOR; SO BE PRESENT AND HAVE FAITH.

When I first met Brendan at that bar in Baltimore, I had no idea the critical role he would play in my life. As our time together went on, I didn't know that all the little moments we had together were just micro-lessons in life that would hold the key to my finding happiness again after he was gone. We can never know what life is preparing us for. We can only trust that it is preparing us for something that we need and from which we will ultimately benefit.

Next time you find yourself with a recurring challenge—the co-worker who drives you mad, the disillusion you experience after a failed relationship—ask yourself why this challenge keeps returning for you. How can you be present in your current situation, and what are you meant to learn from the experience? How can it prepare you for the life you want to lead? No matter how small the obstacle is, it can teach you something about yourself.

Heather

CHAPTER 7

★ ★ ★

Tuesday, November 9, 2010

My knock at the door came at 3 a.m.

I was in a deep sleep, and when I first heard the rap at the front door, it felt far away. I was still coming out of a drowsy haze, so I didn't recognize the noise for what it was. In fact, I thought the knocking noise I was hearing was part of a dream. Eventually, I realized that the sound was real and it was coming from my own front door.

Obviously, I wasn't expecting company at that hour, so I hesitated before answering. I got to the door and looked through the peephole to see three sharply dressed Marines standing together. Immediately, I had a sinking feeling in my gut. My husband, Rob, had deployed to Afghanistan six weeks earlier. It was our third deployment together and I knew that the appearance of Marines, in uniform, at your home, was rarely a good thing. Then I remembered something I had heard in a meeting I attended for spouses of deployed service members, and it gave me some hope.

"If you receive a notification," a family readiness officer had instructed us shortly before Rob left, "two to three Marines will come to your house no earlier than eight o'clock in the morning."

I recalled sitting with other military families at the meeting, where we learned important things we would need to know to get through the next seven months. A strict protocol governs how families are notified of a loved one's death, we learned. Remembering the readiness officer's words calmed me. If this were bad news about Rob, it wouldn't be coming for another five hours, at least.

I wondered how long the Marines had been standing outside trying to get my attention. After concluding it was unlikely they were there for Rob, I figured they were there to ask about where another Marine's family lived. I felt sorry for whoever they were planning to visit later that morning. Regardless of whom they were seeking to visit, I knew that they were bringing bad news for someone. I had been half asleep just a moment ago, but I was wide awake now.

I'd spent the night before like any number of other ordinary nights at home. I cooked dinner and settled in to watch some TV before going to bed. I don't remember what I watched, but I know that I made a veggie casserole that evening because I remember returning home weeks later to find the leftovers in my fridge.

For now, however, I was still trying to wrap my brain around what was happening. I opened the door and welcomed the men inside. I only had a minute or so to process what was going on. There had already been several casualties on this deployment, even though it was early on. Two of our good friends, Second Lieutenant James Byler and Second Lieutenant Cameron West, had been injured, and I knew that Rob had lost members of his platoon.

Receiving news of our friends' injuries in the weeks prior had been a rude awakening. It had hit way too close to home, and I wasn't ready for more bad news. I ushered the Marines into the living room and sat down on the couch, feeling anxious. In just a moment, all my questions would be answered.

One of the Marines served as notification officer, and he began his formal, scripted speech telling me that my husband, Lieutenant Robert Kelly, was dead.

"On behalf of the president of the United States," he began...

The rest is a blur. My head fell in my hands and

my brain shut down completely. I heard the remainder of the script as though I were under water. Something about the "honor of the duty Lieutenant Kelly had been performing"; something about how he had "sustained injuries from an IED* blast that resulted in the loss of his leg"; and some formal closing where I caught only the phrase "extend our deepest sympathies." And then, silence.

When he finished reading the speech, the notification officer looked up and stared at me, I imagine waiting for a storm to erupt. I felt the gaze of the two Marines on me and then saw them look to the chaplain who had accompanied them. I don't think they were quite sure what to make of my reaction—or rather, lack of reaction. There was nothing on the surface to observe from me. I was in total shock; I didn't offer any bellowing screams or agonized cries; no torrent of questions for them to field.

I think they would have much preferred if I had. Instead, I sat dumbfounded, staring straight ahead. All that stood between me and them was a deep, quiet sadness that made me feel empty.

The news that Rob was dead didn't seem real, and yet it was real enough to leave me hollow. Unlike some people, I didn't immediately conclude that there must

---

*   Improvised explosive device.

have been some mistake; that this notification couldn't have been meant for me. I knew this wasn't the kind of thing they were going to screw up. Rob was gone forever, and that was clear to me.

I'm not sure how long we sat in silence, but I imagine the three gentlemen were painfully uncomfortable with it.

"Let's get you a blanket," one of them finally suggested. He went to a nearby room, retrieved a blanket, and draped it over my shoulders. I continued staring straight ahead. I think the other Marine offered me something to eat. I'm sure they were looking for any signs of life from me, but I simply didn't know what to say or do; and neither did they, it seemed.

Rob and I had had a few deployments under our belts. I wasn't nearly as naive now as I had been on his first deployment, when I was still in college and he was fresh out of boot camp. But even still, no one believes they're going to receive the knock at the door. You don't believe it could ever happen to you. No one does. And no matter how many times I had scoured the internet and news channels looking for any sign of Rob on the casualty lists during his deployment, there was simply no way to prepare myself to receive the one piece of news I feared the most. There was nothing to be said, so I said nothing.

There are few specifics about the encounter that are solid in my mind. Hearing that my husband had lost his leg is certainly something I'll never forget, as is the painful silence that enveloped the room afterward.

One thing that I do remember in acute detail was the ridiculous pajama T-shirt that I was wearing. Even through the unimaginable awfulness of that day, I still look back and laugh at what I was sporting when the Marines came and woke me up. It was one of my favorite shirts, and I wore it often. It was a vibrant turquoise color and was emblazoned across the front with the saying, I CAN HARDLY CONTAIN MYSELF. Rob hated that shirt, and he always gave me a hard time—in a light-hearted way—for wearing it. I loved that shirt and its deadpan, sarcastic message. But I also can't think of a more incongruous article of clothing to be wearing as you receive the news that your husband has been killed in a war half a world away. I'm sure that Rob got a good laugh out of that as he looked down on me. I'll always picture him saying, *You just* had *to wear that one to bed that night, didn't you?*

"So, what now?" I finally asked when I found my voice. "Who else knows?"

My casualty assistance officer looked relieved when I broke the silence. He informed me that my in-laws, Rob's parents, had been made aware at the same time I was, so there was no burden on me to share the news. Rob's father, General John Kelly, was then an active-duty Marine and a senior leader in the Marine Corps. As commander of Marine Forces Reserve and Marine

Forces North, he would see the names of casualties when he arrived at the office.

That would be a terrible way for a father to learn of his son's death in Afghanistan, so the Marines had sent his friend and fellow Marine, General Joe Dunford, to notify the Kellys at their home in Washington. Dunford was the assistant commandant of the Marine Corps at the time and had known Rob's dad for decades; the two men had served together as junior officers when they were in their twenties. Because I was three hours behind in California, that meant I would be learning at the same hour, which explained the strange timing of the visit.

I was glad to hear that my in-laws were with friends and that they were receiving the support they needed in that moment. I immediately thought of Rob's siblings and wondered if they had been told.

I want to see Johnny, I thought. Rob's brother, John, was also a Marine and was stationed at the Marine Corps Air Ground Combat Center in Twentynine Palms, California, which was less than three hours away from me. Once I heard the news, the only thing I wanted to do was talk to him. He was the closest member of the Kelly family geographically, and we'd always had a good relationship. He wasn't Rob, but he was the closest to him that I could get.

His parents must have spoken with him already, because I never even had to pick up the phone. Johnny had jumped right into his car and driven to my house, where he sprang into action as soon as he arrived. He talked with the Marines in the house and then with his family back east, trying to learn as much as he could. He slowly brought me out of my state of shock and sat with me that entire day. I can't remember what we talked about as we sat in the living room, but his mere presence was comforting and a real lifesaver.

He helped me prepare to head to the East Coast by calling a pet-sitter who would care for my two cats for a few weeks while I was gone. He took care of all the random details that I couldn't bear to deal with at the time and freed me up so I could pack. I remember not having the slightest idea of what to take with me.

On some level, I knew I was packing for my husband's funeral, but actually selecting something to wear and putting it in my suitcase made the news so real and undeniable. Packing a funeral dress felt like accepting that Rob was gone forever. I settled on a black dress that I loved. I'd only had the chance to wear it once before, when Rob was at The Basic School, a Marine officer training school. I couldn't believe I'd be burying my husband in that same dress.

That afternoon, I flew home to New Jersey with my casualty assistance calls officer, or CACO. Major Chris Gibson had been assigned to help me navigate my husband's funeral affairs. He came neatly dressed in his Alphas, the dark-green Marine uniforms that hark back to World War II–era dress. I'm not sure if it was because of the medals that adorned his uniform or what, but he got held up at airport security, where the Transportation Security Administration (TSA) agents made a big scene about needing to pat him down. To distract myself from cursing the TSA, I gave myself a little pep talk to prepare for the flight ahead.

Okay, Heather, you are not *going to cry in front of these strangers,* I told myself. *It's a long flight from Orange County to Newark, and you're going to keep it together. If the flight attendant asks you if you want a soda, you're going to smile politely and tell her you'd love a Coke. Just act like everything is normal.*

Despite my gloom, I found that it wasn't all that difficult for me to hold it together. Nothing makes me feel more uncomfortable than getting emotional in front of strangers. There were plenty of times when I broke down those first few days, but I was dead set on no one being around to see it. Not even my mom, if I could avoid it. Even when I called my mom that morning from California to tell her Rob was dead, I found myself getting frustrated when she reacted by wailing over the phone. I can't explain it, but I felt that it was no time for such displays of emotion. It felt cheap and pitiful. It was time to set my jaw and power through. And that's what I intended to do.

We touched down in Newark at around 10 p.m. Chris stayed at a nearby hotel and I returned to my childhood home, where my parents were still living. I have no siblings and my house was rarely filled with activity anyway, but in those first few days, it felt especially quiet. It was almost eerie to go back and sleep in my childhood bedroom and see photos and other reminders of life from what seemed long ago. I saw keepsakes that I had collected from grade school and high school and felt disconnected from that life. I was a new person now. I had shifted from being a dependent child to being a capable grown-up to being a wife. And now, at twenty-six years of age, I was a widow. I couldn't make sense of it.

I was relieved when it was time for my parents and me to leave New Jersey and travel to Washington to be with Rob's family. I just wanted to be around people who knew and loved Rob and who could make me feel a little closer to him. At the time, my in-laws were living at the Navy Yard. Just down the road from them, at the end of a tiny street of Colonial houses, was a small hotel, which contained several small apartments. My parents, aunt, and friend Melissa stayed there with me until November 22, the day of the funeral.

Rob had told his father that, should anything happen to him, he wanted to be buried at Arlington National Cemetery. Rob and I had talked about the subject, but it never got far. As I said, no one *really* believes they'll be forced to make these decisions one day, particularly not for their twenty-nine-year-old husband. So I never pushed the issue.

I do remember that on one occasion, however, shortly after we were married, I had watched a moving documentary about the cemetery. I vividly remember seeing footage of brokenhearted families seated cross-legged on the grass, gently touching the headstones of their loved ones.

"You have to be cremated, Rob," I remember telling him later that night. I couldn't get the images of those families out of my head.

"I don't think the Catholic Church permits that," he responded. "No, I'm not going to be cremated." And that was the end of it. It was hardly a discussion then; not because we didn't want to hash things out, or because either of us was trying to be difficult. It was just so far from our minds at the time, as a newlywed couple. There was no reason to push to resolve a moot disagreement. I mean, what were the chances anyway?

"Okay, fine," I told him. But I was still so affected by what I'd seen. My heart broke for those families, who would go on to spend birthdays and anniversaries on a picnic blanket talking quietly to a tombstone that would never talk back.

"I mean, I understand. It's just that I don't think I could leave you somewhere, Rob. I know I sound like a crazy person, but I need you with me."

He gave me a warm smile and told me I didn't have anything to worry about. It was easy for both of us to shrug it off and chalk it up to a difference of opinion.

And here I was now, faced with that exact scenario. In a few short days, I would put my husband in the ground, and I'd turn my back and walk away, leaving him there. I'd have given anything to have him back in that moment; to give me a kiss on the forehead and convince me I had nothing to worry about.

As we worked through all the logistics of the burial, Johnny was once again my saving grace. Gallows humor proved to be my earliest coping mechanism to get through the day, and thankfully, Johnny jumped right on board. I remember sitting with him and my father-in-law at the funeral home making final arrangements for Rob. The funeral director was busy up-selling us some ornate and lavishly decorated guest book that he insisted would *only* be fitting for so noble an occasion.

The guest book was large and leather-bound, emblazoned with an imprint of an eagle soaring across an American flag or some such nonsense. I never pictured myself selecting what to wear to my husband's funeral at the age of twenty-six, much less what kind of decorations should go on his funeral guest book. Plain brown was fine with me, and I'm pretty sure Rob didn't care one way or the other. Johnny clearly sensed I thought this was as ridiculous as he did.

"You know what Rob really would have wanted, Heather?" he whispered to me with a playful smile. "He would have wanted you to ride in on an elephant. Let's take this whole event to the next level, right? Let's do it right." Johnny knew how Rob loved to embrace my crazy whims, but of course this proposition was a stretch by anyone's standards.

I had to suppress a laugh because the timing would have been terrible. The mental image of me atop a giant elephant amid a somber funeral ceremony was too much. In the days that followed, the elephant joke took on a life of its own between the two of us. I'd feign bratty outrage over the idea that my husband's wishes weren't being honored and that I wasn't getting the elephant I so *justly* deserved. Johnny reminded me of the *Simpsons* episode where Bart finds himself in a similar situation after choosing an elephant as his prize for a radio contest, and then exhibits supreme indignation when no such elephant materializes.

When I was sure no one else could hear me, I'd gently pound the table with Veruca Salt–like scorn and "shout" (in a hushed tone of course), "Where's my elephant!?" An outsider looking in probably would have been horrified. But I was grateful Johnny was there to imagine something so absurd in order to lighten an otherwise very heavy time.

Later on, back at the house, we continued the joke, talking about it in the company of a few Marines. They were eager to fulfill the wishes of a fallen hero's family, and God bless them, they actually half-seriously discussed getting me to the Washington Zoo. I think they may have even placed a phone call to the zoo to arrange for me to pet an elephant, which they figured would be a close second to leasing one for the day. Ah, Marines. No better friends in the world, no worse enemies. They probably would have stolen us an elephant if we had asked them to.

I was so grateful to have a chance to smile in that room at the funeral home, if only for a few minutes. The whole affair was so surreal, it bordered on the absurd. Imagining grandiose and preposterous final requests of what "Rob would have wanted" became our morbid joke for the week and helped us get through an otherwise utterly depressing set of circumstances. Rob would have loved getting in on the action. I could just see him sitting at the table with us: a giant grin and eyes sparkling with mischief, adding to the ridiculousness by piling on more and more outlandish requests.

I thought about Rob's bright smile and wondered what he looked like right now. Would the casket be open or closed? That sobering question brought me quickly back to earth. I remembered the words of the notification officer who recounted "the loss of his leg" that Rob sustained during the blast, and I shuddered. It was a horrific thought.

Shortly before Rob deployed, when we went to sleep at night, I remembered taking comfort in knowing that he was only inches away from me in bed. We were never really the cuddly type. He liked his space and I liked mine. But when it came time for him to deploy for several months, I wasn't so concerned with my personal space anymore. I'd reach for his arm at night and breathe a sigh of relief: *He's here, everything is okay.* To think about Rob's arm or leg or any part of his body detached from the whole shook me in a way I'd never been shaken.

Dark humor was one way I sought to escape the sickening feelings that stayed with me. Johnny and I went hunting for humor wherever we could find it, but our opportunities were limited. And anything that began lighthearted inevitably ended with a cold, heavy thud when we faced the reality in front of us. We did the best we could, though, and we tried to imagine Rob sitting alongside us at the table doing the same.

A few days later, we held Rob's funeral Mass at a church on Fort Myer, adjacent to Arlington National Cemetery. Afterward, in a procession, we walked behind a ceremonial caisson, which was essentially a horse-drawn wagon that looked like it should have held a Civil War–era cannon.

Instead, it held the flag-draped casket carrying my husband. I walked with my CACO toward the front of the procession, and we continued for a mile or so until we reached Section 60 of Arlington National Cemetery, where Rob would be lowered into his final resting spot.

At the time of Rob's death, I didn't know the stories of Travis Manion and Brendan Looney. But as fate would have it, Rob would be buried just a few rows from them;

I would meet their family members; and they would change my life.

Before Arlington National Cemetery became Rob's permanent residence, I'd been there just once before. I don't come from a military family, and I was unaware of all the rich tradition that surrounds the cemetery.

My first trip to Arlington was unforgettable, though. I was in college at the time, and Rob, who was three years older than me, had already graduated, joined the Marines, and completed a deployment to Iraq.

I was on spring break, and I visited the Washington area to spend time with Rob and his parents, who were living there. I'll never forget how handsome Rob looked in his green Alpha uniform that day. Rob and I started with a visit to his father in his office at the Pentagon, and then the three of us made the short trip to Arlington. Rob wanted to pay his respects to Lance Corporal Dimitrios Gavriel, a friend with whom he had served on his deployment to Iraq. Rob had always looked up to Gavriel and had told me about him on several occasions when Gavriel was still living.

"This guy was working on Wall Street, making tons of money," I remember him telling me when he first met Gavriel. "He was a stud wrestler who went to Brown and had this incredible career. Then 9/11 happens in his home city, and some of his friends are killed. So what does he do? He up and enlists, sheds forty pounds off his wrestling body, and becomes an infantry Marine.

He's starting out as a lance corporal at twenty-eight with guys a decade younger than him. How freaking awesome is that? He's like straight out of a movie."

Rob was in awe of this man. I think he was too modest to acknowledge the fact that he himself had done basically the same thing, enlisting after he graduated from college. He probably would have argued that he had been influenced to join the military by his brother and father, so it wasn't as impressive when he elected to follow that route. He would have found some way to make the compliment about somebody else, anybody but himself.

Regardless, Gavriel represented the pinnacle of character to Rob. He had everything that Rob admired: selflessness, courage, toughness, competence, and humility. To Rob, that's what it meant to be a Marine. Gavriel and Rob had met when they served together in Iraq. It was Rob's first deployment and he didn't share a ton of it with me, but I could tell, when he returned, that it had changed him. After Rob's return, I learned that his company had lost thirteen Marines on that deployment. I was only a junior in college then, but day by day I was learning more about the military and the way that it was shaping Rob before my very eyes.

I looked at Rob, I suppose, the way he looked at Gavriel. Everything he did was so unselfish, so purely motivated. The idea that I could owe something to a country that afforded me so much—that thought simply never occurred to me. I never once considered joining the service, or even doing any service-oriented work for my career.

Not that I could have handled the physical challenges or emotional hardship that comes with being a Marine anyway; but even if I had been able to, that type of sacrifice was the furthest thing from my mind. Learning more about Rob's respect for military service helped me to know him better.

That day, I was curious to visit the hallowed grounds of Arlington with him and his father and to get another peek behind this mysterious curtain.

As soon as we set foot on the cemetery grass, I knew that this place was special. We stood solemnly at Gavriel's grave, and I felt passersby stare at us. Rob and his dad were both dressed in their uniforms, and people began to take notice. I felt so proud to stand beside them. Their dignity and reverence were contagious to those of us who stood nearby.

I remember glancing around at the endless sea of crisp, white headstones. I felt so humbled by all the men and women who had given their lives in defense of our country. On the way to Gavriel's grave, I wandered past a grave site and was shocked to see a photo of a handsome young man taped to the headstone. He was smiling at the camera as he showed off a newborn baby.

The more headstones I looked at, the more I learned about the people buried beneath them. I started noting the death dates engraved on the stones. A lot of them were my age, give or take a couple years, when they died. They were brothers and sisters, husbands and wives.

In addition to taped photos, mementos had been left that revealed the personalities of their fallen heroes: a colorful drawing torn off a legal pad; a shot glass of whiskey resting precariously on top of a grave marker; a Chicago Bears flag planted in the ground. These were real people who had lived real lives. This shouldn't have surprised me, but it did. It was easier for me to imagine some long-gone veteran of World War I, with a charming, but comparably ancient, black-and-white photo resting against a rugged tombstone. I was only twenty years old at the time, but that visit to Arlington matured me in a way I still can't quite describe.

As I walked slowly behind the caisson, leading a funeral procession I wanted no part of, I thought back to that first visit with Rob and his father. I never dreamed that, five years later, I'd be back to bury my husband.

At the very least, it was comforting to know that Rob would be in the eternal presence of Marine buddies like Gavriel.

When it came time to say goodbye after the burial— just as I had anticipated—I didn't want to leave Rob behind. I wanted so badly to keep him with me in some physical way. It didn't feel right for him to stay there in this unfamiliar place, and for me to be forced to continue on without him. I thought back to the e e cummings poem we both loved:

i carry your heart with me (i carry it in
my heart) i am never without it (anywhere
i go you go, my dear; and whatever is done
by only me is your doing, my darling)

I gave Rob that poem on a little card before he deployed, and it brings me peace to know that he had it with him in his final moments of life, or so I believe. When he died, all of his personal effects came back to me in a chest, neatly packed and cataloged in great detail. And I mean, *all* of his personal effects— right down to a receipt for a bottle of Gatorade he had purchased a few weeks prior. In a small, velvet bag, I received the rank bars that had adorned Rob's uniform at the shoulders. They were slightly charred from the blast that killed him. I received his freshly washed and folded uniforms. Like the rest of his belongings, they had been preserved with painstaking attention to detail. The one thing I didn't receive, in fact, was the laminated copy of the e e cummings poem I had given him before he left. I'm certain he had it with him when the IED went off and it disintegrated in the explosion that claimed his life.

Though I hated to leave Rob behind at Arlington that day, I was comforted to know that he carried me in his heart, and I carried him in mine. *I am never without it*, I thought as I left the cemetery that day. *Anywhere I go you go, my dear.*

There's a line of that same poem that goes, "I fear no fate, for you are my fate, my sweet." I truly believe that. There's not much I can say about an afterlife, or if there even is one. But if there is, I hope you can find me wherever Rob is. That line of thinking, while poetic and beautiful in many ways, has plagued me at times. Rob was my best friend. It was hard for me to imagine a life without him in it. After all, his fate was my fate. And after he was killed, there were months and months when I honestly couldn't have cared if I lived or died.

I wouldn't say I was suicidal, and I certainly never took any measures to hasten our reunion, but I wouldn't have minded if something or someone else had. On occasion, I would ask myself, *If you got hit by a bus on the highway today, would you care?* For a long time, my answer was no. As far as I was concerned, time simply couldn't go fast enough. What had once been an exciting life full of potential was now a punishing sentence I simply had to endure. I had turned twenty-six a month before my husband died. Life should have been a blank canvas I was excited to leave my mark on. Instead, it was an hourglass containing grains of sand that I was waiting impatiently to run out.

After Rob's burial, I returned to our home in California accompanied by my mom. She stayed with me for several months as I worked to get back on my feet. It was strange to be back at the base, even though I no longer had any real connection to military life. I remember one evening hearing a noise at the front door and looking through the peephole. It was dark outside.

Almost immediately, I felt that same sick feeling in my stomach that I had experienced the morning I received the news that changed my life forever. It was just a physically sick feeling of dread. Something as simple as gazing out the peephole at my doorstep and seeing the porch light fall in a similar pattern was all it took to transport me back to that moment when I learned about Rob. And it was a feeling that I never wanted to experience again. I knew that I needed to move past that moment to get my life back on track, but I had no idea how.

Thank God my mom was there to push me along. She forced me to actually do something with my time, when all I wanted to do was watch it disappear. Mostly, I wanted to sleep the days away, because being unconscious and dead to the world was the quickest and least painful way to pass the time. But my mom instituted a plan: Together we would accomplish one thing each day.

In the beginning, that meant simply taking a shower. Even that effort seemed daunting. And when I completed the goal, I was free to go back to bed. As time went on, the tasks got a little more involved—spending an hour at the Social Security office to collect some fifty-five-dollar check in Rob's name; going to the Verizon store to cancel his phone contract; making calls to close his credit card accounts.

As soon as I finished the task or returned home from the errand, I would head straight to my room for another nap. I'd sleep until dinner and then, as soon as we had eaten, I was back in bed. What else was I going to do with my day? I felt no compulsion to visit with friends or go out to dinner or take a walk. I wasn't living in those days. I was merely existing.

Eventually, I evolved from being empty and apathetic into being angry. At first, I was angry about the set of circumstances that had stolen my husband away from me. At the time of Rob's death, he was on a foot patrol with several other Marines, crossing a canal. The IED he stepped on was barely detectable. These sorts of death traps aren't meant to be obvious, of course, but this one was especially treacherous because it had been there long enough for grass to grow over it; and thus, it was easily missed by Rob when he went to take a step.

Maybe this little detail would have made someone else feel better; perhaps it would have brought confirmation that the event, while tragic, was unavoidable. There's no way he could have noticed that IED. But that was not the case with me. I found it infuriating. You mean to tell me that that bomb had been planted there for months—maybe even years—and had been passed over by American after American, and Rob just happened to be the one to step on it? It brought me no peace at all to know that my future had been ripped from me on account of such a hapless brush with chance.

And when I was done being angry at the situation, I directed my anger toward others. I was frustrated living back in Marine Corps base housing. I felt so out of place. I was planted among all the active-duty families who were in the midst of the typical military life cycle of work-ups, deployments, and reunions, and I felt disconnected from all of it. I went to meetings with the other wives as it came time for their husbands to return from Afghanistan, knowing full well mine wouldn't be among them.

I thought it would make me feel connected to a community, but it had the opposite effect. I felt alienated and annoyed. I went back to work at my job in retail at a Bath & Body Works store and found myself telling off customers in my head. *You people have no freaking clue*, I'd think to myself. I'd try to keep my composure when a customer went on a five-minute tirade about how it was an "absolute disgrace" that we didn't keep more warm vanilla sugar body lotion in stock, or when a shopper bemoaned the fact that I wouldn't accept an expired coupon. It took every ounce of my discipline not to shake them and tell them that, if these were their biggest complaints, they didn't know how good they had it.

And finally, after I had exhausted my anger toward others, I directed it toward myself in the form of guilt. I never worried that I could have done more to prevent Rob's death or to let him know how loved he was, but guilt was, nonetheless, an inescapable part of my grieving process. It would hit me in the most subtle and unexpected ways.

For example, about six months after we buried Rob, I decided to treat myself to a new comforter for our bed. I selected a bright pink-and-orange floral quilt from Garnet Hill to brighten up a room that held so many dark memories as of late. It was a Lilly Pulitzer design with cheery flowers on one side and buzzing bumblebees on the other. I figured my room could use a little refreshing. I found it on final sale. It was nothing extravagant, but it was fancier than the items I usually bought at that time in my life.

When it arrived in the mail, I was excited to open it and see how it looked in our room. But as I lifted the cardboard flap and peeked inside the box, I felt sick. What was I doing? How could I be so frivolous? I felt guilty for feeling happy about something so shallow. I was angry at myself for trying to move on from or revise the life and home Rob and I had built together. I even felt guilty about the money I had used to purchase the quilt.

When Rob died, I received what was in his bank account, as well as the standard-issue compensation from the military's life insurance. The idea of using his money at all—let alone to buy something so silly and unnecessary—nauseated me. It may sound irrational, but purchasing that blanket felt like I was endorsing, or somehow accepting, Rob's death; like I was okay accepting money and new furnishings in exchange for the lives we were meant to spend together. Looking at the blanket, I felt I'd purchased something with blood money. I was disgusted and upset with myself.

I never quite got over that feeling. Because it had been on final sale, I was unable to return the blanket, but to this day the quilt remains in its original packaging buried deep in my closet. I have no plans to bring it back out, though I've tried to pawn it off on friends on several occasions.

These years without Rob have been trying. When we were in our early twenties and newly married, life was nothing but a flurry of possibilities. Would Rob make the Marines a career? Would we move again? Would we live abroad? Would we have a family? What unforeseen obstacles would we roll up our sleeves and tackle together? We didn't know, but we were excited to find out.

The not-knowing was never scary for us, certainly not at that age anyway. After all, *uncertainty* was just another word for "possibility," and that felt thrilling.

When Rob was killed and all that possibility disappeared in an instant, the uncertainty of what life would be like without him was a weight I couldn't bear. There was no life without Rob. There was no plan B. "I fear no fate because you are my fate," and all that. So what happens when one half of a couple bound to the same fate forever makes an early exit? This was never part of the design.

At this moment, there sits on my desk at work a framed image that I look at daily. It's two skeletons holding hands. Below them are the words, 'TIL DEATH DO US PART IS FOR QUITTERS. And I'm no quitter. Rob and I promised to love one another for the rest of our lives. He kept his end of the deal, and I intend to keep mine. It's only in recent years that I've started to be able to imagine a life for myself beyond the one that Rob and I built together. I've slowly permitted myself to have that thought, without becoming riddled with debilitating guilt.

The years we spent together were not nearly enough, but they were the best of my life. And I hope, with the years I have left, I can keep some part of him in this world by living the way he did. My friends and family have heard me say this before, but Rob was a just a better person than I was. It's that simple, really. He was less judgmental and more forgiving. He was self-sacrificing, generous, and tons of fun to be around. The world needs more of all those things, doesn't it?

And I can't, for the life of me, figure out why we were deprived of them. Unfortunately, I can't do anything about that. I couldn't have kept my husband from stepping on that IED, but I can prevent the loss of the qualities he had, and the values he stood for. I want to do that for him. I want to bring his spirit of generosity, humor, and warmth to others. After years of struggling, I'm now in a position where I can do that. It took some time, but I made it. And I don't intend to squander the opportunity.

CHAPTER 8

★ ★ ★

The Road Map

Two or three months after Rob died, I was linked up with a financial adviser named Chip Stratmann. Chip, a former Marine himself, came highly recommended by other people in the military community, who assured me that I could trust him.

The quilt incident had left me feeling queasy about anything financially related to Rob's death, and I knew I was going to need to get a handle on things soon. All service members on active duty have term policies issued by Servicemembers' Group Life Insurance.

Within a week or two after a service member dies, beneficiaries receive a lump sum—oddly named a "death gratuity"—to address immediate financial needs. That timing is important, because service members' paychecks stop the day they die. Many families need immediate support to cover rent, utilities, and other bills, and to pay for funeral expenses that aren't covered by the military.

Many young widows, including myself, have no idea how to handle this sudden change in financial status and are desperate for direction they can trust on how to navigate it. Since my husband's death, I've heard stories of many young widows left penniless soon after their husband's death.

In some cases, they mismanage the benefits; in other cases, unscrupulous "money managers" prey upon them—promising one thing and delivering another. As someone who's gone through it, I can say it's nearly impossible to make sound decisions that will affect your life when your world has just been turned upside down.

In those moments of vulnerability, you'll do just about anything you're told you should do, provided the advice comes from someone who indicates he or she has authority on the matter. It doesn't matter if that voice of authority comes from an advertisement that says those pricey shoes are the only things that stand between you and happiness, or if it comes from a scheming predator posing as a financial adviser.

In my case, I wasn't worried about being victimized;

I was more anxious to get the money out of sight and out of mind. It felt dirty to have it in my possession, and I wanted someone else to handle it. Enter Chip Stratmann.

Chip greeted me at his office one day with warmth and what appeared to be an almost paternal desire to see me through this uncertain time. He was well aware of my circumstances and eager to help. We sat down, and he pulled out a thick piece of paper folded several times. He called it "the financial road map."

"The financial road map works just like a regular map, you see," he said as he started to unfold the paper, which did resemble something you'd be given at the visitors center of a zoo or at the mouth of a hiking trail. He spread out the paper and flattened it in front me of me to reveal a panorama of possibilities for my future.

"Now, the base of the map shows you the foundations of your financial future," he said. "These are things like purchasing a car or buying a home that you might want to consider early on. Then, as you move up the map, there are various milestones along the way to consider: whether you want to set aside a personal travel fund, how to plan for the children you hope to have, whether you're going to help finance their college education, all the way up to personal investments and your eventual retirement."

Each milestone was accompanied by an empty box that encouraged me to imagine the kind of future I wanted to have and enter it into the space.

I stared at the milestones on the paper and the progression they created toward old age. I knew this resource was meant to take complicated, abstract decisions and turn them into something concrete and understandable. I'm sure it did for many people. It probably gave them a sense of control over their lives and a clear vision for how to rebuild their lives. But I felt none of that. Every milestone laid out on the sheet of paper in front of me was another reminder that I would miss out on the life I had planned to have.

A house? For whom? It was just me. Where was I supposed to live anyway? The Marine Corps brought Rob and me to California. Was there any point in staying here? And kids? Nothing could have been further from my mind than caring for children. Retirement? I couldn't even wrap my head around that. I pictured myself with gray hair and a couple bottles of Trader Joe's wine, alone on my couch with no one for company but my cats. *I hope I'm long gone before my life comes to that,* I thought.

Chip was patient and thorough in his explanation of the road map and didn't seem to sense how disconnected I was from the exercise.

"So today," he went on, "I thought we'd talk about your goals, and we'll enter each goal into the proper place on the financial road map. So..." He took a breath and smiled at me. "What are your goals?"

I stared at the map in silence. I looked up at his

expectant face and welcoming smile then back down at the map. I had nothing.

"I, uh, I don't have any," I said slowly.

"Okay, no problem," Chip responded. "That's okay. It can be overwhelming to look at it all together. Maybe we just take one at a time. Where do you think you'd like to be five years from now?"

In five years, I would be thirty-one. It sounded like a lifetime away, and yet it also sounded too young an age. Time wasn't passing quickly enough. There was likely still a lot of life ahead after thirty-one, but it felt like a prison sentence. I wished I was going to be eighty in five years to just get life over with, faster.

"I don't know," I said.

"Okay," Chip said slowly. He was willing to try again. "Do you think you'll want to buy a house someday?"

"I just, I don't know."

We both stared at the map laid out on the table between us. The silence seemed interminable. It was a terrible feeling to look straight down the barrel at the dismal years ahead for me. I had nothing to say. There was no plan anymore. Rob was the plan, end of story. He was the only plan and now he was gone. *I have no goals because everything in my life has been taken away. I don't have one single thing to put on this stupid road map. What do I want to do with my life? I want to get through it. That's it.* That was the only goal I could think of.

After sitting in silence for what seemed like several

minutes, Chip decided to call it. "It's okay," he said. "We can always come back to the financial road map." He refolded the paper.

I left that meeting feeling defeated. There was a time when I would have loved an exercise like that. Rob and I would have gladly sat down and stumbled our way through the road map, knowing full well we didn't have the slightest idea what we were doing. Even big decisions felt lighthearted with Rob. He made everything fun and made the future something to look forward to. In fact, planning for the future and building anticipation toward it was, in many ways, the cornerstone of our relationship. Much of our time was spent apart, dreaming about the next time we'd be together again.

I was practically a baby when I first met Rob. I was seventeen years old, a young freshman at Florida State University, who wouldn't even be legal to vote until a few weeks into the first semester. He was a senior with a winsome, outgoing personality that made him easy to be around. He was friends with my cousin Matt, who also attended Florida State, and who was a large part of the reason I'd decided on a college so far away from my home in New Jersey.

It was late August and I'd just arrived on campus in Tallahassee. Matt rented a house off campus near the football stadium and invited me over for a tailgate party before the game. Rob was there, along with two other friends whom he had invited down from Virginia, where he had spent much of his childhood.

As the party got under way, Rob appeared preoccupied with his visitors, but as soon as Matt introduced us, Rob's attention shifted to me. We laughed and joked around the whole night. I remember being flirtatious and stealing his baseball cap at one point and wearing it around for a portion of the evening. I thought he was cute, but our first interaction was innocent, playful teasing, and I didn't put much stock in it. I was happy to take it all in and experience this new thing called "college."

Soon after the party, Rob found ways to "accidentally" run into me. On one occasion, I called Matt to come over and help me hang a shelf on my dorm room wall. Rob happened to be standing near Matt when he answered the phone, overheard the conversation, and insisted it was a two-man job and that he would gladly assist.

On another occasion, Rob offered to take me to Target under the pretense that he had some things to buy to prepare for the beginning of the school year. I had mentioned that I had a mild obsession with the store and sometimes just walked around to see what new merchandise they were pushing. I jumped at the opportunity. We spent some time chatting and strolling up and down the aisles until I reminded him that he had actually come there to buy something.

"So what do you need?" I finally asked.

"Oh right. I almost forgot." He grabbed a wooden spoon off a nearby rack. "Here it is. This is what I need."

Another time, Rob and Matt engineered a surprise double date. Now, "surprise" and "double date" should never go together. In theory, it should have been a complete disaster, but Rob was effortlessly fun and charming and, of course, it wasn't.

In that instance, Matt asked me if I wanted to grab a cousin dinner with him one night, and I accepted. When he pulled up in his green Jeep to pick me up, Rob was in the front seat, beaming. I hopped in the back, confused, but pleasantly surprised. We then went to pick up another girl, who looked just as surprised as I was. I'm sure she, too, had thought she was having dinner with Matt alone, and hadn't expected Rob and me to accompany them.

Throughout September, I found myself unexpectedly spending more and more time with Rob. I remember going over to his house one evening. We fell into watching a marathon of *The Real World: Las Vegas* until 2 a.m., talking about whatever silly ideas popped into our heads. He hadn't even tried to kiss me that first month, but we spent nearly every waking moment together. I was quickly growing attached.

By my birthday in early October, we were officially dating. In fact, we were rarely apart. I'd spend mornings goofing off with Rob and his friends, and at some point in the afternoons, Rob would drop me off at my dorm or take me to class. I had an acute case of Fear of Missing Out in those days and would come up with any excuse I could to skip class and spend more time with him.

We hated to say goodbye to one another, even for just a few days at fall break. At the Christmas holiday, he went back to his parents' house—which was now in California, since the Marine Corps had moved his family across the country—and I returned to New Jersey.

We were excited to get back to one another for the spring semester, but the excitement came with a caveat. Springtime also meant that the departure of Rob's father was looming. It was about this time, in 2003, that the Iraq War began, and since Rob's father was active duty, he prepared to deploy to a combat zone.

I'm sure that was a stressful time for Rob, but he never let on to me. He was in his senior year, preparing to graduate with a history degree and unsure of what his next move would be. He watched his father head off to war, and he returned to carefree college life in Tallahassee with his freshman girlfriend.

There must have been some cognitive dissonance there, but he was always patient, fun loving, and warm to me. I'm sure he worried occasionally about his father, but he knew how capable the man was—as both a leader and as a Marine. More than feeling worried for him, he felt awe. Rob mentioned to me once or twice that he had expressed concern to his father about his safety, but his father had always shrugged it off.

"Nah, I'll be fine," the patriarch would assure his family as he waved a hand dismissively. "Sure, things get messy out there, but I'm always thrown clear of any danger." It was tough to argue with such confidence, and I could see why Rob so admired his father.

Somewhere along the way, Rob inherited that same cool self-reliance that his father always exhibited. He sounded as though he thought he was invincible, and I had no doubt that he was.

Before long, a life of service started to call Rob's name, too, just as it had for his father and brother before him. Shortly after graduation in May, he decided to take a Saturday and visit a recruiting station to learn a little more about what military life would be like for him. He settled on a nearby Coast Guard recruiting station, a rebellious deviation from the Kelly family pedigree of Devil Dogs—a nickname for the Marines.

When Rob approached the building that Saturday, he saw that it was closed. He turned and started to walk back to his car. As luck would have it, a Marine Corps recruiting station was located just next door, and a Marine recruiter had been watching Rob's every move. When he saw Rob turn away from the Coast Guard building, the recruiter decided to try his luck. He poked his head out the front door and yelled over to Rob.

"Do you...uh...want to talk to someone?" he ventured.

Rob's servant heart couldn't resist the opportunity,

and less than forty-eight hours later, Rob had enlisted in the United States Marine Corps. He was told he'd be shipped off in September to boot camp for three months at Parris Island, South Carolina. Rob did the math and realized he was being granted one final hurrah in Tallahassee: a full summer with no job, no worries, and just enough savings to pay for rent and cheap beer. He planned to take full advantage of his freedom before he was stripped of it at boot camp.

I, on the other hand, already had a plane ticket—purchased by my parents—back to New Jersey. When the semester ended, I gave Rob a tearful goodbye and headed back north. When I arrived in New Jersey, I couldn't even feel excited about reuniting with my parents and high school friends. I just missed Rob. I begged my parents to let me move back down to Florida to spend the summer with him.

"We just bought a ticket to get you here, Heather," my mom said. "We're not buying another one to send you back."

I didn't have enough money to purchase a ticket on my own, so I continued to plead with them. I remember desperately crying to my mom.

"You have to let me go back to see Rob. He's joining the military now, and going to boot camp soon, and I don't know if I'll ever see him again," I wailed—or something equally uncalled for and dramatic. I must have worn her down, though, because she relented.

I owe my mother a debt of gratitude for that one, because that summer after freshman year was probably the best three months of my life. Some of my fondest memories with Rob are from that time. I don't remember the moving process from New Jersey to Florida. I only remember being so excited to see him and not wanting to spend a single minute apart from him. We did nothing but goof off the entire summer.

Our lives were such a joke. We neither worked nor took any classes. I spent my afternoons at the pool on campus watching Rob and his friends do outlandish tricks off the diving board. We spent our evenings at the movies or at the mall, or enjoying five-dollar all-you-can-drink beers at Irish Pub or AJ's Sports Bar & Grille.

Rob didn't take his preparation for boot camp terribly seriously and rarely, if ever, worked out. By the time he packed up his things in September, he was almost looking a little full in the face. It was such a fun, carefree time in our lives, and neither of us wanted it to end. When it finally did, Rob and I said our goodbyes and prepared to endure the first of many separations.

And so began a love affair with detailed calendars and daily countdowns. Moments after I kissed Rob goodbye and watched him drive off to basic training, I searched online for a weekly calendar for Marine Corps recruits. I reviewed what activities he'd be up to each week for the next eighty-four days and made a personal calendar so I could follow along and cross out each week as it passed. The final destination was graduation, and time just couldn't move fast enough. Twelve weeks sounded like an eternity, but at least it was something I could get my arms around. It gave me something to look forward to.

Over the next several years, this became nearly the only way I would measure time. I didn't think in terms of days of the week or months of the year. I thought in terms of how many more days until I saw Rob. At any given time, a friend would ask when I'd see Rob again, and I'd be able to give an exact number.

There was a direct correlation between my calendar and my mood. At thirty days out, I was frustrated. At fifteen days out, I started to get anxious. At ten days out I allowed myself to become excited, and at five days out I was beaming. There was simply no better feeling in the world than one day out—except, of course, for day zero.

I was so excited counting down the days until I would see him at graduation from boot camp that I never stopped to think about what would happen once graduation was over. I met him on Parris Island to celebrate with his family, and it wasn't until then that it finally dawned on me that the clock resets after each celebration. I had thought we were done, but it turned out we were just getting started.

It's a good thing I loved the process of crafting

countdowns, because they were about to become my entire life. Anyone who's managed a long-distance relationship knows the drill: Your life becomes an emotional game of ping-pong between joyous reunions and painful separations, with anticipation serving as the momentum that keeps the cycle in motion.

After we jumped the boot camp hurdle, Rob was stationed at Marine Corps Base Camp Lejeune, North Carolina, and I returned for my sophomore year in Tallahassee, a fourteen-hour drive away.

In no time at all, I knew the exact number of days until spring break, when I would go to visit him, or until the next long weekend, when he would come and visit me.

Before I knew it, I was counting down to June, when Rob would visit with me one last time before he left for his first deployment. Outside of mutual love and respect for one another, our relationship was anchored in this experience of anticipation. It made our lives fun and exciting. When we weren't savoring our time together in the present, we were anticipating it in the future. We imagined the experience in great detail: which restaurant we would go to, which fancy drink we would order, what we would talk about. Imagining was half the fun.

It was only nine months between the day Rob reported to boot camp and the day he touched down in a combat zone in Iraq. Long gone were the carefree days of creative spins off the diving board and cheap pitchers of beer at AJ's. We were both growing up quickly.

During that first, seven-month deployment, Rob had his first encounter with the ugliness and complexity of war. It affected him, but he preferred to share the details of it with his father rather than with me. I recall him getting choked up one night at dinner, talking about Gavriel and other men they'd lost.

It caught me completely off guard to see my happy-go-lucky Rob become emotional. I'd never seen him like that. But he tried not to dwell on the sad parts of deployment. He reserved only the humorous or playful parts for our conversations: tales of the disgusting rats he found sleeping in his tent with him or quirky stories about the other Marines he served with.

The intensity of his experiences was very real, however, and those experiences, coupled with the distance that separated us, caused our relationship to mature pretty quickly. There was no doubt from either of us that we wanted to be together forever. We talked about marriage frequently, but I still had my senior year of college to finish, and I wasn't going to drop out just so we could get married.

And Rob had another deployment coming up, so we decided to rely on our calendars and countdowns to get us through the short term until we could make long-term plans for our lives together.

By the time I graduated FSU in the spring of 2006,

Rob was completing his work-ups in preparation for his second deployment. Rather than return to Iraq, Rob would be spending his second deployment at sea: seven months on a marine expeditionary unit, or MEU, which meant he would be part of a small reaction force aboard a ship, sailing through the Strait of Gibraltar, bouncing around the Mediterranean, and sailing in the Persian Gulf. The idea behind these deployments was to have an amphibious unit of Marines available to respond quickly to any crises on land or on the water.

Sometimes the unit responds to nearby natural disasters, and other times it provides support for combat missions. During that deployment, Rob's ship would see both types of action, but by and large it was much more relaxed than his previous deployment to Iraq had been.

After finishing his work-ups, Rob went to New Jersey to spend a few days with me and my family during his pre-deployment leave. We wanted to celebrate my graduation and clock as much time together as possible before it was time for him to go, so we made plans for a quick getaway to nearby Atlantic City. As we passed by the jewelry store of an Atlantic City casino, I pointed to a shiny, diamond ring.

"That's the kind of ring I'd like, Rob. Just like that one."

We'd talked about marriage dozens of times before, but never with this level of specificity. Rob had told me that his MEU would pass through Dubai and that he heard he could get really cheap diamonds while in port there. I figured it couldn't hurt to give some not-so-subtle hints about my jewelry preferences before he shipped out and made any decisions independently. He looked at the ring behind the glass and smiled, but he wasn't going to make things *that* easy for me.

"You're going to have to write that down, Heather. I'm never going to remember that." I sighed and made a mental note to come back to it another time. Little did I know, he already had my engagement ring packed away in his suitcase upstairs.

It was such a beautiful day in May, so I told Rob I wanted to go to the beach and take some pictures. As we were walking along the shore, we found large scallop shells to serve as props for our photo shoot. No one else was around, so we held the shells up and took a series of photos where each of us was wearing our makeshift "mermaid bra." I couldn't stop laughing and snapping away at this tough-guy infantry Marine modeling a shell bra on the beaches of Atlantic City.

"Wait, take a picture with my camera," Rob insisted.

This was, of course, before the days of smartphones with professional-grade cameras built in, so we were each lugging around a digital camera to capture the mini-vacation.

"I'll just send you a copy," I told him. "I've got it on my camera."

"No, I really want one on mine. Can you just take one on mine?" He was insistent, but I couldn't understand why.

I picked up his case and reached inside for the camera, but what I found instead was a little box. I opened it to reveal a beautiful diamond ring. My heart nearly stopped. I pulled it out and looked at Rob, but he was more frozen than I was. He didn't get down on one knee and he didn't open his mouth to say another word. He just stood there like a mannequin. I think he was too nervous to do anything but wait for my next move. I'm not even sure if he was breathing at this point.

"So..." I started nervously. "Um...What finger does this go on?"

I racked my brain for a less awkward way to inquire whether I was being proposed to or not. It was just indirect enough to save me some dignity if it turned out this wasn't a proposal of marriage. I mean, who wants to be presumptuous in a situation like that? Imagine thinking you were being proposed to when, in fact, you weren't. What if it was just a promise ring he was gifting me? And I shouted "Yes, of course!" and jumped into his arms, only to have him explain to me that I'd grossly misunderstood? Or worse, what if it was just a pretty piece of pre-deployment jewelry to remember him by when he was gone? No way. I wasn't willing to risk it.

My lack of an immediate and enthusiastic response was probably Rob's nightmare. He continued to stare at me, mouth ever so slightly agape. In my defense, the poor man wasn't doing himself any favors. There was no bended knee, no question being posed, no verbal indication at all, in fact, that this was a proposal of marriage. I was working with very few clues, so "What finger does this go on?" was the best response I could muster. He looked terrified, but finally he managed to find his voice,

"Well," he said, "it's an engagement ring, Heather."

Phew! That was a close one. I felt a giant wave of relief wash over me. That was followed by a tidal wave of complete and total joy when I got to jump into his arms after all. I couldn't wait to be Mrs. Heather Kelly.

We took our excitement down to DC, where we celebrated with Rob's close family and friends and prepared ourselves for another seven-month separation. And of course, as always, there was another countdown on the horizon until his return. And when we hit that one, there would be a rush of other exciting things to imagine: wedding plans, career discussions, vacations, moves, and the like. We saw our lives unfolding like a road before us and we couldn't wait for all the landmarks along the way.

Once Rob departed for deployment in June 2006, I became happily distracted with making wedding plans. Now I had two exciting countdowns to track: one for Rob's return in early December 2006, and one for our wedding a few months later, in June 2007.

I don't know that anyone would claim that "time flies" on a deployment, but that one came pretty close. I was busy trying on wedding dresses, visiting possible venues, collecting addresses for invitations, picking out registry items with my mom at Crate & Barrel, selecting a color palette, and coming up with a list of "must play" songs for our DJ. The countdown flew faster than any I'd remembered. Rob returned and I was ecstatic. Greeting each other after that second deployment, we knew we couldn't wait a second longer to make our commitment official. We had planned for me to move down to North Carolina after our wedding in June, but that felt eons away. While I was visiting him there after deployment, he finally turned to me one day and asked, "Why can't you just move here now?"

I thought on it for a second, and it seemed so obvious.

"You're right. Why wait until June? You're back now; we've waited long enough. What are we waiting for, at this point?" Anticipation was fun and it had its moments, but we were tired of always waiting for something. I moved in February to North Carolina, and we went in March to the local courthouse for a marriage certificate. We couldn't wait any longer. Rob and I were both in jeans, and we called his friends Greg and Andrew to serve as witnesses.

When we arrived at the courthouse, we saw a guy turning himself in. He was quickly cuffed and ushered away. Rob and I couldn't help but giggle to one another at the absurdity of it all.

We then stood in front of a man who was wearing a bright-red NORTH CAROLINA STATE polo shirt who was about to officiate our marriage.

"Y'all are jokin' and laughin' like this ain't 'bout to be legal," he chastised us in a thick Southern accent.

"Oh no," Rob said. "It's not that. We're getting married in June. This is just a formality."

"Well, why didn't ya say so?" He quickly skipped to the end of his binder and said, "I now pronounce you man and wife."

Rob and I kissed and then headed to a friend's house to celebrate as Mr. and Mrs. Kelly. We were already looking forward to the next countdown: three more months until we did this again in front of friends and family, but next time, with a little more grandeur.

Rob and I had created an exciting road map for our relationship, one that included significant mile markers for us as a couple. It had begun with a carefree year in Tallahassee; shifted to a period of growth on Parris Island and at Camp Lejeune; traversed oceans and gained gravity in Iraq; and circled back for an engagement in New Jersey and an unexpected wedding down south. We liked to imagine where else our road map would take us, and all the exhilarating countdowns we could anticipate along the way.

However, the road map that Rob and I had imagined

together early in our marriage looked very different from the one Chip placed in front of me at our meeting a few months after Rob's death. The basic principles were the same, of course, but everything felt different. Both road maps encouraged me to take a concrete look into the future; imagine a life that would feel fulfilling; and make decisions in the present that would build toward that life.

Both road maps began clean and unmarked, waiting for my decisions about how to imprint and color them. But while one elicited feelings of anticipation, excitement, and possibility, the other inspired nothing but emptiness and dread.

My entire relationship with Rob had been defined by milestones we intended to reach together: from graduations and homecomings to personal and professional celebrations. We loved daydreaming about what life would be like for us three months, six months, and twelve months out from wherever we were at that point in our journey. Most of our excitement revolved around short-term goals: making it through basic training; reuniting after deployment; counting down to our wedding date, and then to our first anniversary.

But we were just as happy to imagine our long-term goals as well: a trip to Europe, a possible career in teaching for Rob after the Marine Corps, a home, a family.

It wasn't that long ago when a look toward the future was what got me out of bed every morning. And here

I was in Chip's office, my entire future ahead of me, and not one single thing to look forward to. No goals, no hopes, no expectations. The anticipation was gone. All that was left in its place were apprehension and disappointment.

I was in a rut when I left Chip's office and returned to my house on base. I pulled into the drive to my neighborhood full of active-duty families, and I wished so badly to be one of them, preparing for the return of my loved one, and rediscovering the long-lost feeling of anticipation. I knew I had to find my way out.

I remembered my mom's principle of picking one thing and focusing on that. I thought back to when taking a shower had been nearly impossible. Within weeks I was closing out accounts and completing complex paperwork. Now I was taking meetings with a financial professional. It was a baby step, but it was something to be proud of. *Okay, what's one thing?* I thought. *I can do this.*

At the bottom of the financial road map were the basic features involved in establishing oneself financially: a house, an automobile. I figured I'd start there. My car was pretty dependable, so I wasn't worried about that. But I loved the idea of moving off base. I didn't fit in there anymore anyway. I was in my mid-twenties and working at a mall bath store, so the last thing I thought I'd be doing was negotiating the sale of a house. But why not?

Patiently, Chip Stratmann guided me through the entire process, and less than one year after Rob's death, I was a homeowner. It was a bittersweet accomplishment to tackle on my own. But as with everything I do, Rob was at the center. It was his life insurance, in fact, that I used to purchase the home—and this acquisition felt totally different from the pink blanket fiasco. That purchase had felt frivolous and insignificant, like I wasn't acknowledging the gravity of what it meant to maintain my husband's legacy. Like I was squandering.

The home, on the other hand, was a personal achievement. I was setting goals again. I was making healthy decisions for my future and taking ownership of my life. I was becoming independent. And rather than feeling disgust or guilt about benefiting from my husband's loss, I felt grateful to him. He had provided me this special gift and was looking out for me—always.

The distinction between a Lilly Pulitzer blanket and a new home is, of course, completely arbitrary. The guilt that one fed and the pride that the other inspired were constructs that I had invented. There's no inherent goodness or badness in either. They're just things.

But during my first year without Rob, that was how I saw them: one negative and shameful; the other positive and encouraging. Looking back now, I see the difference between the two for what it truly is: a creation of my own design. It's funny how time allows us to do that. Only with the passage of time could I gain the perspective that two similar experiences could elicit completely different emotional responses from me.

It's just like the countdown calendar and the financial road map. They weren't so different after all. Both tools gave me the opportunity to imagine the future and anticipate what my life would be like when I reached the final destination. But at the time, one was thrilling, and the other depressing.

Perspective changes everything. When I was barely twenty-six, I hoped that the sand in my life's hourglass would run out quickly. I didn't know what I'd be missing if it did.

I'm several years out from the loss of my husband, First Lieutenant Rob Kelly. I think about him every day. He came into my life bringing me humor and kindness and love, and he left me with the gift of perspective. And that perspective has re-taught me the wonderfully precious gift of anticipation. Sometimes I wonder what advice I could give to others who find themselves struggling. I doubt whether I'm able to give a lot of value. But I can promise them that they will find things to look forward to once again if they allow enough time to pass.

YOUR DREAM MAY BE TAKEN AWAY FROM YOU
TOMORROW. DREAM ANYWAY.

When my seventeen-year-old self met charismatic Rob Kelly at FSU in 2002, we dreamed of spending our lives together. It was a fun dream that occupied the greater part of our adult lives every day thereafter. As the years went on, the dream remained, but it evolved to become more mature and complex, and we adjusted it to whatever our circumstances happened to be at any given time.

We imagined our reunion after deployment; we imagined hosting parties as a married couple at our new house; we imagined holidays with our future family. We played that dream out in minute detail and gleaned as much pleasure as we possibly could from it. We wrung it dry. And then, one day in 2010, I buried my fellow dreamer and was left to dream alone.

Obviously, there was no landmark on the mental road map I had created for myself that accounted for this. No part of the dream involved losing my husband at so young an age. But sometimes navigating life is like driving through a snowstorm: You can only see ten feet in front of you. It's scary and treacherous, but you know what? It's doable. You can make the whole journey that way. You may not know what awaits you fifteen or fifty miles down the road, but that shouldn't stop you from dreaming about how wonderful it will be when you get there.

If Rob and I had known that fate would separate us so early in our marriage, I don't think our dreams would have looked any different. We still would have had that carefree summer in Tallahassee. We still would have spent our time apart marking down the days until our next reunion. We still would have committed our lives to one another.

Anyone's dreams can be ripped away in an instant. And, believe me, it hurts like hell. I'm not going to pretend it doesn't. But dream anyway. The joyful anticipation those dreams bring you will far outweigh the pain their absence leaves behind. After all, anticipation is half the fun.

BE PATIENT WITH YOURSELF. YOU ARE A WORK IN PROGRESS.

When I consider what the horrible experience of losing Rob has taught me, I think a lot about anger and the lessons I have learned in regulating my emotions. To the outsider, it may seem like I over-regulate at times. I'm not outwardly demonstrative of my grief, so when emotions consume me, it's a short-tempered anger—not a weepy sadness—that dominates. And anger can take many forms. For me, it has shown up as frustration with customers at work or feelings of guilt about my desire to move on from Rob's death. Slowly, I'm learning to let go of these negative emotions.

I imagine there's a better version of myself, five or six years down the road maybe, who will be able to say honestly that all the anger has disappeared. I like to imagine a future me who has accepted the reality of this experience and has made peace with it.

I am not yet that person. I still get angry and disappointed. I still question why Rob had to be the one to step on that IED, why he had to be there at all. It's at times like this that I remind myself that grief is a process, and so am I. Every day is an evolution, and I allow space and forgiveness for the times I fall short of being the person I'd like to be. Any one of us would quickly dismiss the faults of a friend whom we knew was struggling. It's important that we show the same sort of mercy toward ourselves.

FINALLY, DO ONE THING—TODAY—TO SET YOURSELF UP FOR SUCCESS TOMORROW.

Just one little thing. It doesn't matter what it is; it just matters that you do it. Maybe you have such intense phobias that you can't stand to leave your house and socialize at the neighborhood block party. Fine, don't even try. But do something. Water your garden, take a stroll around the block. You have to start somewhere.

For a long time, I thought that sleeping my days away and praying for time to pass quickly was the best thing for me. I honestly thought it was the best thing, because it allowed me to get closer to my ultimate goal, which was…what? Dying eventually, I guess? It sounds grim to put it that way, but that's subconsciously where I was headed. I was so intent on simply managing the pain and getting through life that I forgot that life is a journey and not a destination. Committing to do one small thing each day that pushed me toward my goal was eventually what reminded me.

We are not on this earth simply to endure. We are here to live. Find one small thing each day that reminds you that you are alive. Bake cupcakes. Pick up dry cleaning. Go to a coffee shop and look at people. Find a moment to step outside of your grief and struggle in order to focus on a simple activity. Eventually, the activities will become ever-more complex, and before you know it you're living without reminding yourself that you have to. Pretty soon after that, you begin to enjoy it. Finally, you rediscover joy and anticipation. And your life is all the richer for it.

★ ★ ★

Old Friendships and New Anniversaries

No one loved celebrating milestones quite like Rob, so that became an integral part of our relationship, and gave us even more to look forward to and get excited about. Rob and I were married for only three and a half years, but we managed to have three wedding ceremonies in that time: our first one at the courthouse in North Carolina, our big church wedding with our families to follow, and then a vow renewal ceremony three days later during our honeymoon in Las Vegas. Each of those ceremonies evokes so many memories, some sweet and romantic and some that make me giggle. We didn't get the lifetime together we had hoped for, but we made sure to cement those vows to each other—over and over and over again.

It's not just milestones that make a relationship special. It's the everyday activities that make up a life. After so much time apart—long-distance dating, military training, deployments—the mundane stuff of life felt extra fun, simply because Rob and I were together.

Life felt perfect when Rob got stationed at Camp Pendleton and we moved from the East Coast to Southern California. Some of my favorite memories are of the Sundays we spent there together. We'd get up, make a big pot of coffee, and relax a little as we eased ourselves into the morning. Rob loved to make himself a big breakfast on the weekends, and he was almost ceremonious in the way he cooked the bacon and eggs and piled everything high on his plate.

Most Sundays, we had a routine. We would go to the barbershop so Rob had a fresh haircut for Monday morning (you know how Marines are), eat lunch at In-N-Out Burger (a SoCal staple; we loved it when we first moved out west), and usually hit Trader Joe's to purchase groceries for the week.

We loved perusing the aisles for fun, new snacks and sweets, and Rob would search for anything with coconut. Depending on the season, we'd end our Sundays by watching some of our favorite shows together, like *Mad Men* or *Dexter*, and cooking dinner together. Little mundane errands to the grocery store or our burger dates to In-N-Out are some of the most cherished memories I have of my time with Rob. There was nothing terribly exciting about these trips. They happened once every seven days. But spending that time together is what made them fun and special.

After Rob was killed in 2010, I thought I'd never have another thing to look forward to in my life. I didn't think I'd derive joy from the simple sweetness of the commonplace ever again. I remember, when my mom was staying with me in California, after Rob died, she suggested we go to Disneyland.

It was my first Christmas without my husband, and I was grateful for her suggestion to make a depressing time of year a little less depressing. I'm a nerd for all things Disney, so I figured if, nothing else, it would be a good distraction.

I was wrong. When we got there, whatever excitement I had been able to muster dissipated quickly. I realized I had been right to think there was nothing in life to look forward to, not even a visit to one of my favorite places on earth. I remember my mom kept wanting to take pictures of the trip and I was insistent that I didn't want any photos of myself.

What are we even documenting things for anymore? I wondered. What was the point? For whom were we saving these images? There seemed to be no point in recording moments that would never be worth reflecting on anyway.

I've tried to make a case that the experience of anticipation is key to overcoming grief and struggle. That proved true for me.

But how are you supposed to recover emotions like joy and excitement when you're in so dark a place? Losing Rob was a loss like no other. When you lose your husband, everything changes. And I mean everything. The way you eat dinner changes. The way you buy food changes. Who you dance with at a wedding changes. Your sense of personal safety and security changes. There's nothing like it.

Everything I had envisioned and planned for was gone the moment those men knocked on my door. I didn't just lose my best friend and partner in life, I lost my entire future. And nothing could have prepared me for it.

At the end the day, it's been my friendships that have led me out of the darkness. Without them, I have no idea where I'd be. Friends can't replace the love of your life, but they can and do remind you that life is still worth living. Friends go on adventures with you and commiserate when all you want to do is complain.

One of those friends proved to be Melissa.

Melissa and I met in 2007. Rob and I were newly married at the time and we had just moved to Quantico, Virginia, where he was about to go through schooling to become a Marine officer. He had been an enlisted Marine for four years already, and when he decided to renew his contract for another four years and become an officer, he had to undergo more training and instruction.

Once in Quantico, I got a job as a manager for a Bath & Body Works store. On my first day on the job, I attended an all-hands meeting with all the store's sales personnel. It was fall and we were meeting to prep for the onslaught of holiday shopping.

When I arrived at the staff meeting, I spotted a friendly-looking brunette who was toting a Longchamp purse with a Coach scarf tied around the strap; she was chatting with everyone in sight. In 2007, an ensemble like that represented the absolute height of fashion forwardness. I wanted to get to know this girl more. Fortunately, I had my chance soon after, when Melissa and I started working together regularly on the sales floor.

Technically, I was her supervisor, but it never felt that way. We clicked automatically as equals. She made our shifts so entertaining; I'd never imagined I could have so much fun selling bath products to strangers.

Almost a year after we had begun working together, I mentioned to Melissa offhandedly that my birthday was coming up in October. I was turning twenty-three. When I left work on the afternoon of my birthday, there was Melissa, standing in the parking lot next to her car, carrying a giant sign and waiting for me. She had been blasting "Happy Birthday" from her car stereo for so long that her battery had died.

We laughed hysterically at the ridiculous predicament we'd somehow found ourselves in, and we searched for someone who could offer a jump to two giggling girls and a giant HAPPY BIRTHDAY sign. Eventually, we found someone. That predicament sealed our relationship and, to this day, we still think of my twenty-third birthday as our "Friendversary."

She's been with me through every step of my journey. When Rob and I lived in Virginia, Melissa would come over for slumber parties, so I didn't have to spend the nights alone when he was out training in the field.

When Rob deployed to Afghanistan, she visited me in California so I wouldn't have to spend my birthday alone. She was there searching casualty lists with me just weeks before I received the fateful knock at the door.

She was one of the first people I called when I learned of his death. When I traveled to Washington to lay him to rest, Melissa was the one who picked me up and took me shopping to find a black purse to match my funeral dress.

I'd never been one to show emotion outwardly, but I had to channel my sadness somewhere, especially in the first few months of being alone.

Usually, it came out in the form of a 2 a.m. email to Melissa in which I wrote my deepest, saddest thoughts. She was three hours behind me in Virginia, and when she woke up to one of those emails, I'm sure she worried about whether I'd made it through the night.

We never had that kind of intense exchange of emotion in person or on the phone, and Melissa never pushed me to. She knew it wasn't my style. She was the patient recipient of all my darkest feelings. She simply absorbed them and accepted them. That was exactly the show of support that I needed. She was also the first person I called when I wanted to pawn my Lilly Pulitzer quilt off on someone. I couldn't return it and I also couldn't bear to look at it at the top of my closet anymore.

"No thanks, Heather," she said. "That thing is way too loud. It's never going to match anything in my house—or anyone else's for that matter." Brutal honesty, another sign of a best friend. Melissa's candor is at least half her charm.

She's been a constant; one of the truly good things in my life when I had very few good things to think of. She's the friend who keeps sunshine in my heart on even the darkest of days and reminds me that life is still good.

Wherever I was, she fielded those scary, late-night emails with patience and quiet concern, and ultimately, she pushed me to learn to appreciate life's little joys once again.

She even helped me rediscover the magic of Disneyland.

I was three years out from having lost Rob, and I was ready for an adventure to take me outside myself. I saw something advertised about a series of half marathons through the Disney parks, which are located on the East and West Coasts. If you completed a Disney-themed half marathon on each coast within a year, you got a special commemorative medal. That proved to be enough incentive for me to give it a go. I called up Melissa and pitched her the idea of us taking five mini-vacations together by running five half marathons together in various Disney parks.

"What are you getting me into, Heather? Can't we do the vacations without the running?" She was appropriately skeptical.

"Oh, come on. I'm going to sign you up. It will be fun." Melissa would teasingly drag her feet now and again, but with enough nudging, I knew she'd always jump on board. Being open to joining an adventure, even if reluctantly, is the mark of a true great friend.

Over the next year, from 2013 to 2014, Melissa and I traveled from Orlando, Florida, to Anaheim, California, in silly costumes of famous cartoon duos. We played everything from Snow White and the Evil Queen to Mike Wazowski and his sidekick Sulley, of *Monsters, Inc.*, fame. We trotted with Tinker Bell, pranced with princesses, and did the Dumbo Double Dare (a 10K and half marathon in a single weekend), ending each race with a well-earned glass of wine and a Dole Whip.

Or two or three. We were never fast, but we weren't out to compete. We were simply there to enjoy the show and nourish a friendship that had been years in the making.

In 2014, we celebrated our Friendversary once again, but decided to do it up big this time. I was turning thirty. It was the first time I was reaching an age that was older than Rob would ever be, and I wanted to get my mind off things. Rob and I had always dreamed of taking a Hawaiian vacation, so I invited Melissa to make the trip with me.

"Come on," I nudged. "A week on the beach? It'll be great."

At first, it had seemed extravagant, and maybe even a little odd to take a trip like that with a friend instead of a life partner. But the more I thought about it, the more I realized it would have been silly *not* to take the leap. Melissa was one of the closest relationships I had. It was nontraditional and not the way I had imagined taking the trip, but she brought fun and humor with her wherever she went. I needed both.

"I'm in," she said.

And—with that two-word response—Melissa gave me permission to look forward to adventures once again. Time and time again, she has reminded me that it is okay to have fun and that I deserve to enjoy life, even if I don't have Rob here to enjoy it alongside me.

Three years later, we returned to Hawaii to celebrate

our ten-year Friendversary. We always joked that she was my significant other now anyway, so it only seemed appropriate to celebrate these milestones together.

We stayed at the Four Seasons Maui and it felt absolutely opulent. We were celebrating our milestone in the lap of luxury. My mom even had balloons and champagne sent to our room with a note wishing us the happiest of anniversaries. We realized that we may have taken the joke just a little too far that time, because the staff had no idea what the nature of our relationship was, and how they were supposed to be treating us.

"Welcome to the Four Seasons," the front desk agent greeted us at check-in. "And what brings you to Hawaii?"

We looked at each other. "Um, vacation," we responded.

"Oh, how wonderful!" She smiled. "And, er, how do you all know each other?" She was feeling us out.

"We worked together," I told her. She looked at me as if expecting me to say more. I think she was waiting for me to finish, ... *and then we started seeing each other, and now we're in love.*

Former co-workers don't take trips together to the Four Seasons in Hawaii. In fact, I think we were the only couple there not honeymooning. I could understand her confusion. Of course, we got a kick out of that and leaned into the joke whenever we felt we could do so inconspicuously. It could have felt depressing to find myself on a honeymoon with a girlfriend after my husband was killed. But somehow, Melissa made it entertaining.

When I lost Rob, I lost my husband and my entire future, yes. But I also lost my best friend; that special person whom I could have fun perusing the aisles of a grocery store with, or who made a simple trip to a fast-food joint an event worth remembering for years to come. All the pain of losing my husband and my future almost overshadowed the fact that I'd lost a friend, too.

I forgot what it was like to have a partner like that in my life, one who could make even the mundane extraordinary.

For years now, Melissa has served as a sounding board when I think I'm going crazy; a patient listener when I want to lament; and a fun distraction who can take my mind off my pain when I need it the most. She knew me before, during, and after the most defining experience of my life, and our relationship has only grown stronger in the years since.

There was nothing for me after Rob died. Just a dark stretch of emptiness with no end in sight. It was terrifying when I considered that that was all that was left for me in this life. My friendship with Melissa was one of the few things I had to hang on to in those desperate days. And I clung to it for dear life. She stood with me through the rough patches, and because of her, I've been able to recover the feelings of excitement and anticipation that I had thought were gone forever.

This is the beauty of friendship. Friends can't take away the hurt that life throws at us, and good ones don't bother trying. They just sit patiently and hold your hand through the process. They don't try to erase your bad feelings or gloss over your experiences.

In fact, they'll even agree with you when you tell them your life sucks. I mean, let's be honest. Sometimes it does. Why deny it? Believe it or not, it's nice to get that kind of affirmation. It's nice to feel heard. And then, after hearing you, and when they sense that you're ready for it, they infuse excitement and laughter back into what has become a cold, dusty existence.

When they can't drag you out of your house for happy hour, friends will show up on your doorstep with a seven-dollar bottle of wine anyway. A good friend is someone you couldn't keep away even if you tried. And when you're grieving, believe me, you do try.

I consider myself doubly fortunate because the people I have befriended, like Melissa and Rob, aren't just my reality-TV-binge-watching buddies, though they certainly have played that role as well. They also happen to be my role models.

Since my husband was killed, I've met even more of these admirable people. When you're wandering down a lonely road, with no trail blazed in front of you, a good role model can be a critical resource in forging ahead, just as much as a trusted friend is.

It's always easier to move forward when you know that someone else has walked in your shoes and made it to the other side. Just when I thought it wasn't possible for me to move forward another step in my grief, I met a woman about my age who had lost her husband just weeks before I lost Rob.

From what I could see, she was not only getting up every morning and functioning as a real, live human being, but she was also working in a job she loved; was involved in a rich social life that she had created; was finding meaning and purpose after her loss; and seemed genuinely happy. As soon as I talked to her for the first time, I knew I needed to know her secret.

The woman was Amy Looney, a few years before she became Amy Looney Heffernan. And it was my trusty financial adviser, Chip Stratmann, who introduced us. I must have made quite an impression on Chip after the episode in his office with the financial road map. Like Melissa after reading one of my 2 a.m. emails, he must have worried about what my future might hold.

Then one day, Chip was reading an article in the *San Diego Union-Tribune*. It was an op-ed written by Amy Looney, a young widow who had lost her husband, Brendan, only weeks before I'd lost Rob. She wanted to do something positive to continue his legacy. Brendan had been more than "a warrior for freedom," Amy had written. She wanted people to remember him as "an ambassador of kindness" as well, and to preserve that memory she was committing to performing ten random acts of kindness for strangers over the next ninety days in his honor. She was asking the rest of San Diego to join her.

Chip, in all his wisdom, knew I would be able to learn something from this Amy Looney, and he found a way to contact her. He asked if she would be willing to speak with me, as someone who had felt similar pain.

Amy immediately accepted the opportunity to chat. Chip told me that Amy was now working for a military nonprofit organization that supported both returning veterans and families of the fallen. He arranged for me to connect with Amy via phone the week before she was to move to Washington to open an office for the nonprofit, called the Travis Manion Foundation.

I was so nervous going into that phone call. What was I supposed to say? I imagined how the conversation might go: *Hi, uh...I noticed you lost your husband. Me too. Let's get coffee and talk about how miserable we both are.*

I couldn't help but feel that this phone meeting could be disastrous, and I was even a little bitter that I had agreed to participate. At the time, small talk with a complete stranger didn't seem like what I was looking for.

When it came time for Amy's call, I answered the phone timidly. I was greeted by an even-keeled voice that was filled with warmth and authenticity. I honestly don't remember much of what Amy and I talked about that day. I do remember that my uneasiness disappeared in the first two or three minutes and that the conversation became fluid and easy after that. We didn't chat long, but before we hung up, Amy invited me to join an event for the Travis Manion Foundation that was scheduled to take place the following week.

She would already be in the midst of her move east and wouldn't make it herself, but she assured me that I'd have the chance to meet other staff members as well as veterans and families of the fallen who were part of the nonprofit's community. I'd always been on the shy side, and since Rob's death, I had been even less likely to put myself out there in unfamiliar settings, but something in Amy's voice told me I should make this event a priority.

I showed up the following week, knowing very little about the Travis Manion Foundation. It turned out that Amy had invited me to a training session for new volunteers. It was a classroom-style orientation in a room filled with a dozen other people who were all either former military or Gold Star family members like me.

The training was to certify volunteers to serve as mentors to local youths as part of a character-development and leadership program. The concept was simple: Take a group of people who had once been connected with military life and give them the tools to share their stories to inspire the next generation of leaders.

The training began by equipping us with the ability to deliver a presentation to high school students. The veterans would draw from their experiences with military leaders, and the families of the fallen would share stories of their loved ones to inspire young leaders to live with character.

I loved the idea of some young person learning about Rob and wanting to emulate his qualities of humor and kindness. But I was terrified at the prospect of getting up in front of a room full of students to talk about the love of my life. I found the volunteer coordinator during a break and shared my concern.

"Um, public speaking isn't exactly my thing," I explained to her. That was putting it mildly. In fact, I was so uncomfortable speaking in front of a crowd that it had become an inside joke between Rob and me. Whenever I was nervous about attending some military get-together or unfamiliar social event, Rob would jokingly convince me that I was expected to stand up and put on a skit in front of the audience as soon as I arrived. I spared the volunteer coordinator this little anecdote, but I had to make sure she knew where I was coming from.

"Look," I told her. "I really love this program, but there's no way I'm going to be able to be one of your speakers. I want to work with you all, and I love what you all stand for. I'll do just about anything else you need."

"Oh, don't even worry about it." She smiled. "I totally understand. I'm glad you came. I'm sure there's something we can find at the Travis Manion Foundation that fits better for your style. What are you looking for?"

I was a little taken aback by the question because I hadn't really thought about it. I was here because my financial adviser had read an article by some stranger and had set up an introduction with the author. What *was* I looking for? I honestly hadn't thought much about where that initial phone call with Amy might lead. But I felt at home here, among people who understood what I had been through and wanted to see me grow from my experience.

I'm not sure what I had been expecting to find at this meeting, but I had initially thought it might look more like a support group. Looking around the room, I could tell that this was no support group. This organization's leaders didn't just want to acknowledge my loss, they wanted to do something about it. They wanted my husband's legacy to live on in generations to come. And they were asking me to help lead that effort. It was a humbling responsibility.

"Wh-what am I looking for?" I stuttered. "Um, anything really. I'm not much of a speaker, so not that. But anything else. I'd love to help with whatever you guys need help with."

Several months later, I was volunteering weekly with the Travis Manion Foundation. I did odd jobs around the San Diego office, inputting Excel spreadsheets and organizing office materials. It wasn't the traditional way that they liked to activate the Gold Star family members with whom they worked, and it wasn't terribly glamorous, but they met me where I was. I was providing value in a way that felt right to me, and I was learning that I was not alone. I was happy to spend time doing something outside of myself and passing a few hours among people whom I genuinely liked and respected.

When a full-time staff position opened up a few months later, I jumped at the opportunity to interview for the job. I'd been trying to get out of retail for years, and I felt like this nonprofit was going to be my ticket to a purpose-filled career and a whole new life for myself. I'll never forget sitting across the table from the West Coast director of the Travis Manion Foundation. I had gone through the interview process and was about to be offered a job that would change my life forever. As he offered me the job, I felt butterflies in my stomach.

"As for a start date," he said as he thumbed through a calendar, "how soon can you begin?"

I wish I could begin yesterday, I thought to myself. "I can give notice to my current job today, and am happy to begin as soon as you'll have me."

"Okay, then. Let's do two weeks from today. That would be Monday, November 9. How does that sound?"

11/09/15. My first day of a new career would also

mark the five-year anniversary of the day I received the knock at the door. It felt too perfect. I took a deep breath and, silently, thanked Rob. Somehow I knew he was at the center of this new chapter. He was always looking out for me.

"It sounds great," I replied as I shook his hand. "I'm looking forward to it."

I left the office that day knowing my life was about to take a substantial turn for the better. As I drove home, I thought about how far I'd come in the last half decade. It was almost hard to believe there had been a time when all I wanted was for time to run out as quickly as possible. Now I was actually looking forward to what life had in store for me. The previous five years had turned my life upside down. So much had changed, including myself. I had a way to go, but I had learned so many powerful lessons along the way.

FIRST, IF YOU EXPECT TO SEE THE GOOD OR YOU EXPECT TO SEE THE BAD, YOU WILL.

There's a quote by Henry Ford that goes, "If you think you can or you think you can't, you're right." Perspective is everything, and so much of life is subject to becoming a self-fulfilling prophecy. I think the way we deal with grief works in much the same way.

Not long ago, I was perusing items for sale at a small

antiques shop near my home in Carlsbad, California, just north of San Diego. I stumbled on a bar set that consisted of two cocktail glasses, one that said YOURS and one that said MINE. The glasses were accompanied by a matching pitcher that said OURS. There was a time when I would have considered the set sweet, but these days I find it depressing.

I was feeling pretty down about the turn my life had taken, and bitter that little reminders of my grief followed me everywhere I went. I turned a corner inside the shop, and as I did, the song that Rob and I considered our song—"Better Together" by Jack Johnson— began playing on a radio that was sitting on a shelf in a nearby booth. I like to think it was Rob's way of reminding me that he was still with me, that he understood the pain I felt, and that, no matter what, I would never be alone.

It's true. Reminders of our difficulties and sadness are everywhere. We don't usually have to look too hard to find them. But the fact is, reminders of happier times are everywhere, too. And we can feel reassured by them and take pleasure in the little gifts of joy they bring to us when we need them the most. Sometimes, however, we have to be much more intentional about seeking out these little signs.

Last Memorial Day, for instance, I tried to embrace the sentiment of the day by taking a walk alone on a beach near my house. I wanted to reflect on my life with Rob, and call up feelings of gratitude for both the life he gave me and the life I built after his death.

It was a conscious effort to not feel sorry for myself and to cultivate feelings of gratitude and hope in place of the bitterness I sometimes felt bubbling up. As I strolled, I thought about how I was on the West Coast because the Marines had moved us here. Southern California had been good to me. Just as I was thinking about how grateful I was for that move and the life I was beginning to create for myself, I noticed letters on the sidewalk in faded spray paint. Time had worn away their vibrancy, but the words were still clear: I WILL LOVE YOU ALWAYS.

It may sound like a stretch to some, but I believe Rob sends little gifts like this when I am ready for them. His love for me was persistent, sweet, and simple, so it seems fitting that the messages he leaves behind are, too. I never would have guessed that a silly shopping trip to Target for a wooden spoon or a marathon of *Mad Men* episodes after cooking dinner at home could be some of the fondest memories I would have with Rob. In life, Rob taught me to appreciate the simple pleasures of the everyday. In death, he reminds me to look for signs of that same sweet simplicity. Can I say for sure that these are attempts from Rob to communicate with me? Unequivocally, I cannot. But I'm much happier when I view these little moments as gifts, rather than dumb coincidence.

SECOND, HAVE A SENSE OF HUMOR. YES, EVEN ABOUT YOUR HUSBAND'S TRAGIC AND UNTIMELY DEATH.

That probably sounds morbid, maybe even grotesque, to most people, but a sense of humor is sometimes the only thing I have to rely on. When I'm too exhausted to be polite and too hurt to be dignified, somehow I find relief in being just a little sarcastic about my dismal situation.

A few years ago, I went for drinks with a group of young military widows in the San Diego area. Yes, there are several of us, and yes, we hang out together. We even try to find a little lightheartedness in the rough patches we call our lives.

One of my friends at the happy hour, Theresa, does black humor better than anyone I know—even better than Rob's brother Johnny, with his outlandish funeral demands. Theresa's husband was a Navy pilot. After he was killed, she was left alone to care for her two sons— a six-year-old and an infant whom her husband had never met.

If anyone is allowed to voice inappropriate widow humor, it's Theresa. She and I and a few other ladies went to a local brewery and decided to give the feature beer, aptly named "Black Widow," a try. We ordered a round for the table, and the bartender informed us that it was no longer available.

"I'm sorry, ladies," he told us. "But the widow is tapped out."

"You're damn right she is," Theresa shot back without skipping a beat. The poor bartender had no idea how beautifully he'd teed that one up.

Allow yourself to find humor in even the darkest and ugliest of situations. It's a powerful lifeline when your regular coping resources, like patience and gratitude, are depleted. Also, laughing is far more fun than crying.

FINALLY, CHOOSE YOUR FRIENDS AND YOUR ROLE
MODELS CAREFULLY. YOU'LL BEGIN TO SEE
YOURSELF REFLECTED IN THEM.

I love that Rob always had role models. Like many young men, he idolized his dad, and it wasn't much of a surprise when he chose to follow in his footsteps.

But the Marine Corps opened Rob up to so many other role models; friends like Gavriel, who traded in his cushy Wall Street job and Ivy League education for a rifle and a deployment to Iraq. Rob idolized teachers whom he knew and admired, as well as police officers, whom he believed had the toughest jobs. It always made me laugh that, somehow, Rob didn't notice that he was just like all these people himself. He saw them as so far above him. They were gritty and self-sacrificing, and—

somehow—Rob's humility prevented him from seeing that he was cut from the same cloth.

I've tried to take that into account in my own life—by being very intentional about whom I select as friends, role models, and mentors, knowing that one day I may see myself in them, too. Women like my co-workers Amy and Ryan, and my friends Melissa and Theresa— they remind me of what strength looks like and how to maintain humor and grace in the face of adversity.

I remember, when I first met Theresa, I was shocked to learn that she had lost her husband, Landon, only a few years before. There I was, several years out from my own loss, with no small children to care for, and I felt I was barely keeping it together. To me, Theresa was some sage who had this grief thing down pat. She was someone I wanted to emulate.

Things are always much more complicated below the surface, of course, and Theresa later shared with me that she, too, felt she was hanging by a thread at times. I have been grateful to have her, as well as other Gold Star family members, as models of both strength and vulnerability these last several years.

I would advise anyone to find a good role model. Think about the principles you value the most and identify people who live by them. Good mentors don't tell you what to do, they show you. And we can all benefit from their example. And if you can't find a good role model, then be one.

CHAPTER 10

"If Not Me, Then Who..."

B efore my brother, Travis, left for his second deployment—the one from which he didn't return—he spent time with us on the East Coast. During that time, he and my husband, Dave, both of whom were huge Philadelphia Eagles fans, decided to catch a game. They passed a few hours in the tailgate parking lot enjoying cigars and a few beers before heading into the stadium to watch an Eagles victory. It was exactly the relaxed kind of fun that Travis was looking for before he returned to Camp Pendleton and then on to Iraq.

When my husband got home from the game that evening, I asked him how it went.

"Oh, it was awesome," he told me. "So good to spend that time with Trav." Dave seemed to have genuinely enjoyed himself, but he had a quizzical look on his face, as if he was still piecing together some portion of the evening. I sensed there was more to the story.

"Well, there was this one thing," he added after a pause. "As we were leaving the stadium, Travis said something, and I can't stop thinking about it."

This piqued my interest, so I asked Dave to tell me more. He went on to share with me what happened as he and Travis were making their way down a large stairwell toward the parking lot with the rest of the crowd after the game.

Travis's imminent departure had been weighing on Dave all evening, and he couldn't bear to ignore the elephant in the room any longer. He'd tried to put it aside to enjoy the night, but he just couldn't let the entire evening go by and not make some mention of Travis's upcoming deployment. In true Dave fashion, he turned it into a lighthearted joke.

"Hey Trav, I got an idea," my husband said as they stood at the top of the stairwell. "Why don't I push you down these stairs? That way, you'll break an ankle and you won't have to go back to Iraq."

From what Dave told me, Travis stopped and looked at him very seriously. He was calm and focused, with no trace of a smile on his face.

"Look, Dave," he said. "I have to go back. I've

trained for this, and I'm ready. If I don't go back, the Marines will just send someone else in my place. Someone who doesn't have my training or skill set; someone less prepared. I have to go. If not me, then who?"

I think Dave was a little embarrassed at the turn the conversation had taken. He hadn't expected Travis to respond with such intensity.

"If not me, then who..."

I knew exactly what Dave meant when he said he couldn't get the words out of his head. There was a gravity to the phrase that we wouldn't fully understand until Travis was gone. Looking back now, knowing what would happen on that final deployment, those words feel even more powerful. When we re-interred Travis at Arlington, and laid him to rest next to Brendan, we had those five words inscribed on his tombstone.

A few years out from our loss gave my family the perspective to understand that those weren't just words Travis spoke at an Eagles game shortly before deployment. They were words he lived by his entire life. He was always looking for opportunities to step up and do the right thing, stand up for a friend, work harder than the guy next to him, or take the harder right over the easier wrong.

He knew he had something special to offer the world, and he wanted to offer it. He knew he was the only one who could. In the end, when he gave the last full measure of his devotion to his teammates and country, that's exactly what he did. It was only fitting that his generous and selfless spirit be preserved with that epitaph.

Several years after Travis's death, I came across those same five words, "If not me, then who..." in an unexpected place: on another man's tombstone.

I received a note on social media from a young man named Tom Hixon, who had recently transitioned out of the Marine Corps. Tom shared a photo online of the grave site of his recently deceased father, Christopher Hixon, a Navy veteran. The image showed a white headstone similar to the one I've visited a hundred times at Arlington. It had a cross at the top, and an inscription that bore Hixon's name, military service, birth and death dates. At the base of the headstone were those words: IF NOT ME, THEN WHO...

I was intrigued that Tom had chosen this inscription for his father's final resting place and wanted to know more. Christopher Hixon, I learned, was the athletic director at Marjory Stoneman Douglas High School in Parkland, Florida, on a day when the United States experienced the deadliest school shooting in its history. On February 14, 2018, a nineteen-year-old former student tore through the school, killing seventeen teenagers and school staff members, and injuring seventeen more.

When the first bullets were fired, Christopher Hixon was in a nearby building, outside of immediate danger. He heard panic-stricken voices over the radio referring to an active shooter and he left his office and ran toward the fray. He knew he could be of assistance to the victims and wanted to offer help. He didn't think—he just acted. At a time when everyone else was running away from the danger, Christopher Hixon was running toward it.

As soon as he reached the building where the shooter was located, Hixon identified students in need of help and did what he could to shield them from the shooter. In the end, he gave his own life to protect the people around him.

When Chris's wife, mother, and two sons, Corey and Tom, made arrangements for his burial, they wanted to find a way to honor his self-sacrificing spirit. Tom had served as a Marine and was familiar with my brother's story. Tom remembered the five words, now the mantra of the organization we started in Travis's honor, and he knew they captured his father's character perfectly. Chris Hixon had always put the welfare of others above his own, and he died trying to protect those who needed him. If there's a better example of what it means to live by the ethos of "If not me, then who..." then I don't know what it is.

I didn't know the Hixons at the time of Christopher Hixon's death or burial. In fact, it wasn't until I saw the image of his tombstone online that I pieced things together and became familiar with the family's story. I was floored that my brother's words had inspired this family and given them a way to honor their father, husband,

and son as he deserved. It was deeply humbling to know that Travis's legacy of service and sacrifice resonated with others.

I contacted Tom shortly after seeing the photo and asked him to share his story with me. He told me more about his father and what an amazing man and role model he was. His father, Tom told me, had a penchant for guiding the "bad kids." He was drawn to the forgotten teens; the ones who were struggling to stay focused, who exhibited behavioral issues in class, or who acted out when they didn't receive enough love and attention at home.

Chris Hixon always took these students under his wing. At any given time, you'd find one or two students in particularly troubled situations living with him and his family in their home. He would support them until they could get back on their feet. "I just know that my dad could have helped that gunman if he were given the chance," Tom told me.

"If that kid ever reached out to my dad rather than go on this violent spree, I know my dad would have been there for him." Chris Hixon was a protector and a caretaker. He had a heart for struggling youths and he offered support and kindness to see them through difficult situations.

Talking with Tom about his father reminded me of the power of legacy. The legacy our loved one leaves behind—the lessons they taught us, the values they stood for, the contributions they made: All of these things are so much bigger than we can imagine. They are so much bigger than our grief and sadness, and they will far outlast whatever pain we have been forced to deal with during our loss. Had it not been for my brother's death and sacrifice, I would never have met this incredible family. And I would have missed the opportunity to be inspired by the actions of an American hero.

It's a tragedy that men like Chris Hixon—or Travis, Brendan, and Rob, for that matter—should be taken from us at all. But if we must lose their physical presence, then let's make sure we don't lose their spirit. It's incumbent upon us—the living—to keep alive their legacies of character. We have to remember the qualities that made our loved ones who they were—their tenacity, their kindness, their sense of humor—and bring those qualities to others. Because if not us, then who?

Shortly after my brother died, my mother founded the Travis Manion Foundation, with the intent of preserving the legacies of all our fallen heroes, not just her son's. In fact, I'm 100 percent confident that Travis would *hate* that he has an organization named after him. In his mind, when he saved his wounded teammates on that day in April 2007, he was doing his job. He was doing what any Marine has been trained to do and he would have insisted that the mission was so much bigger than his alone. And he'd have been right. Our mission is, in fact, so much bigger than Travis Manion.

When my mom founded the organization in 2007, my dad and I thought of it as her coping mechanism. We knew she wanted to build something positive and powerful out of a grief that was deep and dark, and we were glad that she had that outlet. At the time, we didn't think of it as much more than a distraction or a pet project. We didn't think it had staying power. We should have known better.

The year 2019 marks twelve years since we first opened the doors of the Travis Manion Foundation. Since then, we've supported and empowered tens of thousands of veterans returning from war, and families of the fallen like Amy, Heather, and myself.

Both groups—veterans and survivors—undergo a difficult transition after they separate from a military life during which they may have lost their identity, sense of purpose, and direction. Our goal is to be there as they navigate those difficult waters and to remind them that they, too, have something to contribute to their communities and country.

And if they truly want to honor their loved one's sacrifice, or their own military service, they will carry on the legacies of character of those who have gone before us. The Travis Manion Foundation provides veterans and survivors with the tools to rediscover their purpose. We help them identify the personal contribution they can make, through serving others, and we create a community of individuals to support that effort.

In my opinion, there are two key ingredients to any successful organization. First: a strong mission. Without a clear objective and bright North Star to follow, it's impossible to meet your goals. The success of our mission is due largely to my mom, who set us up with a strong foundation. From the outset, the mission of the Travis Manion Foundation has been to support and empower our nation's veterans and the families of the fallen, and to leverage them as leaders to create stronger communities and a nation built on character. She felt confident that investing in our military community would pay dividends, and her theory has proved true over the past dozen years.

The second critical ingredient: good people. You can do literally anything with a clear objective and good people to execute it. Have you heard the phrase, "The people make the party"? That's not just advice for hosting a dinner. It's advice for life. Surround yourself with people who inspire and challenge you, and I promise you, good things will happen.

My mom must have recognized this, too, which is why she insisted that Amy Looney join the Travis Manion Foundation staff after Brendan was killed. My mom knew that adding someone like Amy to the roster would be a home run.

Shortly before my mom died, she made the pitch. Amy was visiting my mom during the fall before she died. My mom was too sick even to get out of bed during that visit, but she was clearheaded and direct with Amy. "Come work at the foundation," she told her. "You can open an office for us in San Diego."

Amy had been struggling to find a new purpose since Brendan's death, and assisting family members who had suffered what she had suffered sounded like a move in the right direction. The rest is history.

A few years after that, Heather Kelly joined the party. Her mild-mannered humility and friendly warmth made her accessible to everyone who encountered her, and she was the perfect draw for adding more good people to our group. Heather took over in San Diego not long after Amy moved eastward to Washington, where she opened yet another location for the Travis Manion Foundation. TMF is a party, and its people most certainly make it a good one.

It's not just the staff that make the party; it's the community we've built. It's the veterans and families of the fallen who have been empowered by our programs; it's the inspired civilians who stand up as leaders to join our mission. This is our party and these are our people. They are the strongest examples of what our country looks like when it's at its best.

And sometimes at TMF, it's a literal party, as it was in Philadelphia this past December.

Each December, on the Thursday before the famous Army-Navy football game, we host our annual gala. It's an inspiring evening dedicated to celebrating the work that our veterans and survivors are doing in their communities to honor fallen heroes and the ways they are strengthening and unifying our nation. We don our fancy dresses, heels, tuxes, and military dress uniforms, and enjoy dinner together.

We celebrate the company of fellow TMF supporters and listen to inspiring speakers in a chandelier-lit ballroom in a mid-nineteenth-century brick building in Center City Philadelphia.

At this past year's gala, I invited the Hixon family to join us so that we could honor the life of their husband, son, and brother, Christopher Hixon. The work of TMF is fueled by the gratitude we have for those who paid the ultimate sacrifice to our nation, and while Hixon wasn't in uniform at the time of his death, his final act of heroism was something that we wanted to amplify.

The Hixons kindly obliged and traveled to Philadelphia. There's no question that the Travis Manion Foundation community is made up of change makers and leaders, and we love to celebrate that. But the heels and tight collars last only so long on us. Sooner or later, our true, casual colors are bound to come out.

Each year, they do.

At the end of the night, when the formal program has ended, our group treks down the block to the unofficial after-party at Tavern on Broad, a dark, dingy little bar located below street level. At about 10:30 p.m., two hundred people walk down Broad Street in formal gowns and black ties, shivering against the December wind, until we reach the warm, welcoming glow of the bar. By the time we arrive, the bar has usually already been overtaken by a raucous office Christmas party and is bumping Def Leppard. So obviously, we make ourselves right at home. This neighborhood tavern after-party is where you *really* get to experience the TMF community in our element.

Last December, I remember looking around the tavern and taking in a private moment of appreciation for what we had built together these last several years. Everywhere I looked was a reminder of the incredible people who have made TMF what it is today.

I looked toward the bar to see Joel Heffernan with his arm around Amy, his new bride. She was beaming with admiration for her husband, whose face was aglow with the details of a story he was sharing with half a dozen eager listeners.

I then glanced over to the corner to see Heather. She was dancing with Tom Hixon's wife, Ines, and laughing with a small group of military widows who had kicked off their heels and were enjoying the sweet release of bare feet.

A few bars of Journey came over the speakers. As if it had been choreographed, the entire bar stopped what they were doing, gathered closely together, and began passionately belting out the lyrics to "Don't Stop Believing."

There, at the center of the huddle, was Tom Hixon. He revealed himself to be an expert and impassioned Steve Perry lip-syncher, and I could tell this wasn't his first rodeo. Before I knew it, Tom had climbed onto the bar and was imagining his clenched fist as a microphone. He was inviting fellow Marines and other guests of the gala to join him on the makeshift stage, and he offered his hand to each to help them climb aboard.

Well, that didn't take long, I thought. Tom and his wife were welcomed into the TMF family in no time. When I invited the Hixons to join us for an inspirational evening of honoring fallen heroes and celebrating the inspirational work of our members and volunteers, somehow I didn't anticipate that a dive bar performance of Journey would be part of the night. It was a little shortsighted on my part, I admit.

After all, why shouldn't it be? I truly believe that good begets more good; that pain shared is halved, and joy shared is doubled. If any community knows that to be true, it's ours. We've all had different journeys, different experiences of struggle and difficulty. We're all at different stages on the road to becoming the people we want to be, but we share the desire to continue down the path. And we'd much rather do it together than go it alone.

The company we keep is a critical indicator of the attitudes we adopt and the way we see ourselves in the grand scheme of life. I've heard that each one of us is the average of the five people we spend the most time with. If that's the case, I feel very fortunate. Through TMF, I spend my time in the company of people like Heather, Amy, the Hixon family, and thousands of the most inspiring Americans I know. Good begets more good.

After our family lost Travis, I remember receiving a lot of advice on how to navigate grief. I was advised both professionally and casually; I participated both in groups and alone; and the counsel was both solicited and unsolicited. But of all the guidance I received, one moment stands out to me, because it served as a turning point in my grief journey. I was with Amy on this particular occasion, when one well-intentioned grief counselor told us, "You may cry every day for the rest of your life. And that's perfectly all right."

We looked at one another incredulously. We were thinking the same thing: *Um, no. No, it's actually not.*

We left that session trying to imagine what Travis and Brendan would think if we spent the rest of our years tearfully mourning their absence rather than continuing on with the lives we were meant to lead.

We knew there was something else in store for us besides a life of wallowing in sadness. I'm sure the counselor's larger intention was to show that grief was a journey of ups and downs, and that it would never be fully in the rearview mirror.

I wholeheartedly agree with that sentiment. Each

day looks different from the one before it, and I don't know that any one of us could ever claim that we've "conquered" our grief.

But that's not the point of grief, is it? It's not something to be crushed or thwarted. If we try to stamp out the difficulties in our life, all we're really doing is ignoring them. That's not helpful. Instead, we learn to accept and incorporate those difficulties as part of our growth journey. Then we find the courage and humility to allow our struggles to transform us.

As much as we may want to, we can't stick our heads under the pillow when we hear our knock at the door. We find the strength to open the door and address what waits for us on the other side.

Since the days when we lost Travis, Brendan, and Rob, the three of us have wanted only to live our lives in a way that was worthy of their sacrifice. Most people who have received a knock on the door—regardless of the form it took—feel the same. Pain and struggle offer us the gift of perspective. They give us the chance to reexamine and alter our lives for the better. It's up to us to decide whether we take that chance or not.

Loss has a staggering impact on our lives. It can make us cold, fearful, and distant; it can also help us to love more, enrich our relationships, and experience joy and gratitude, uplifting those around us. It can turn us inward, causing us to forever ask ourselves *why* and to blame the world for its unfairness. But loss can also turn us outward toward our friends, families, and communities, and awaken us to opportunities we'd never noticed before.

We've learned that, if we take this latter path to others by channeling grief into service, tragedy can ultimately be our biggest triumph. It can show our true character, reveal the best versions of ourselves. By reminding us of the fragility of human connections and by forcing us to question why we're here on this earth, tragedy can help us serve others and our communities and do other extraordinary things.

We see these extraordinary examples every day at the Travis Manion Foundation, where we're fortunate to have thousands of volunteers who have been through some of the most trying circumstances known to humanity.

We've climbed some of the tallest summits in the world with survivors of IED blasts that had torn off their limbs. We've been into schools throughout the United States and talked with hundreds of thousands of students about the importance of character. We've run alongside double-amputee marathoners. We've traveled to Third World countries to build houses for homeless families.

Loss also gives us insight into the human experience. It can help us to find a new sense of purpose in our lives. For us, finding purpose comes down to two interrelated things—love and service. The crushing pain of our loved ones' deaths reminded us just how capable we were of loving someone, and just how frequently we took it for granted when they were around.

We can't replace the love that we felt for Travis, Brendan, and Rob. But we can recover the deepest expression of that love in service to others and to our communities. In our experience, every time we give away a piece of ourselves—our time, our attention, our story—we find that that investment comes back to us tenfold.

Tucked away in a drawer at home, I keep a literal reminder of my knock at the door. It's a small piece of a metal hinge, worn with age and rust. It was torn from my parents' front door when my mom slammed it in the faces of the uniformed men who were there to tell her that her son was dead.

She simply couldn't bear to face them, and her involuntary and visceral reaction was to try to shut out the pain that was coming for her. This is a tempting response for any of us who have been forced to face loss, pain, or struggle.

It's not something I look at often, but I still can't bring myself to throw away that hinge. It's a sobering reminder to me that a knock at the door is inescapable. It's part and parcel of being human. It may come when we least expect it, and when we feel the least equipped to handle it.

But it's also a reminder of what's possible when we

embrace that struggle and allow it to fuel us, as my mom did. We can't avoid the knock at the door. We can only prepare ourselves to greet it when it comes. When it does, we may respond imperfectly. Such is human nature. But in our imperfection and vulnerability, we also find untapped strength and courage that we never knew we had.

Epilogue

★ ★ ★

It is a bit overwhelming at times to think about how far out our losses become as each year passes. I remember thinking in the early days after Travis's death that I could not fathom hitting the one-year mark, and just like that, one year came and went.

But time has a way of granting a unique perspective. This exercise has led us all collectively to revisit things we weren't sure we were ready to revisit and to share things we never thought we would share.

Ultimately, it has given each of us another opportunity to process the knock at the door. We set out to share our stories knowing that the only way to do it properly would be to allow ourselves to be vulnerable.

Over the past few years, people have told me countless times, "You are so strong. I don't know how you keep it together." It is a nice compliment and one I never tire of hearing, but this book was a way for us to tear down that picture-perfect exterior and let people know that we all fall down sometimes.

We live in a world today where taking the perfect picture for Instagram is achieved by trying several times and using a good filter. I myself am guilty at times of creating an online persona that is completely unachievable, but I think we have all learned, through this process, that true strength is achieved when you can show the world the most authentic version of yourself, no matter how ugly that may look.

We all take a certain pride in knowing we are works in progress. Not having all the answers is the best answer we can give to how we have navigated these past several years, and there is a true beauty in that. Beauty not because we have all been dealt the same cards, but because each of us has played our hands a bit differently with a combination of success and failure.

It was during that *CBS This Morning* interview that the anchor asked me a question about our work at the Travis Manion Foundation and I answered by saying that I felt "blessed" to wake up every day and have the opportunities I have.

As I soon as I said that, I felt awkward, and the look on the anchor's face only added to that feeling. "Blessed?"

she asked. "That is a unique choice of words, given that the work you do is as a result of your brother's death."

I gave a canned response that, luckily, was cut from the interview before the piece aired. I have asked myself many times why I chose that word and whether it in some way diminished the loss I had suffered. The truth is that I do feel blessed. Blessed that I have been granted the chance to continue to walk this earth for another day with passion and purpose.

How many of us get the chance to work alongside individuals who make us a better version of ourselves? That is what Amy and Heather do for me. I thank them for having opened their hearts to share their stories alongside my own, and I am forever grateful to Travis, Brendan, and Rob for bringing us together.

Acknowledgments

There are countless people to thank for helping this project come together.

To our agent, Keith Urbahn, and the entire team at Javelin: Thank you for presenting us with the opportunity to share our story and for your unmatched guidance through this journey.

To our publisher, Center Street, and the entire Hachette Book Group: Thank you for your belief in our story and your incredible support.

To Molly Boyle Bartnick: This book would not be a reality if not for you. Your talent is endless, and our appreciation for your efforts knows no bounds.

To our families and friends: In good times and in bad, you have been there for us. We love you all.

To Travis, Brendan, and Rob: Thank you for giving us the strength to keep going after the knock at the door.

About the Authors

Ryan Manion is the surviving sister of Marine 1st Lt. Travis Manion, who was killed in Iraq on April 29, 2007. His death served as the inspiration for establishing the Travis Manion Foundation, a nationally recognized veteran service organization. Today Ryan leads the foundation as its president, and as a highly regarded advocate for the military community, she addresses national audiences frequently.

Amy Looney Heffernan is the surviving spouse of Lt. Brendan Looney, a West Coast–based Navy SEAL who was killed in Afghanistan on September 21, 2010. Brendan was also the best friend and Naval Academy roommate of Travis Manion. Amy has a master's degree in public administration and serves as the vice-president of the Travis Manion Foundation.

Heather Kelly is the surviving spouse of Marine 1st Lt. Robert Kelly, who was killed in Afghanistan on

November 9, 2010. Serving as the West Region program manager for the Travis Manion Foundation, Heather works closely with veterans returning to civilian life and the surviving family members of those who make the ultimate sacrifice, helping to foster America's next generation of leaders.